An Improvised Life

ALAN ARKIN
an improvised
life *a memoir*

DA CAPO PRESS
A Member of the Perseus Books Group

Designed by Trish Wilkinson
Set in 12 point Adobe Garamond Pro

Library of Congress Cataloging-in-Publication Data

Arkin, Alan.
  An improvised life : a memoir / Alan Arkin. — 1st Da Capo Press ed.
    p. cm.
  Includes index.
  ISBN 978-0-306-81966-7 (alk. paper)
  1. Arkin, Alan. 2. Motion picture actors and actresses—
United States—Biography. I. Title.
PN2287.A685A3 2011
791.43'028'092—dc22
[B]   2010045034

First Da Capo Press edition 2011

Published by Da Capo Press
A Member of the Perseus Books Group
www.dacapopress.com

Da Capo Press books are available at special discounts for bulk purchases in the U.S. by corporations, institutions, and other organizations. For more information, please contact the Special Markets Department at the Perseus Books Group, 2300 Chestnut Street, Suite 200, Philadelphia, PA 19103, or call (800) 810-4145, ext. 5000, or e-mail special.markets @perseusbooks.com.

10 9 8 7 6 5 4 3 2 1

APR 2011

ACKNOWLEDGMENTS

Thanks

To Susan Cohen, my wonderful literary agent who steadfastly refused to let me abandon this project.

To Barry Berg, my editor and now friend, who was endlessly encouraging, supportive and wise and who miraculously made working and reworking this book a joy.

And to my wife, Suzanne, my constant companion, my best friend and my muse. She is also an integral part of the workshops. She organizes them, she takes every one of them and interprets my broken English when I become inarticulate, which is more often than I'd like to admit. Her participation in the workshops is endlessly joyous, rooted in the moment, and without dropping character she becomes a perfect litmus paper when someone else in a scene is either 'playwriting' or making jokes. As a result, when she's up there she has an unfailing ability to keep other participants in the reality of a scene. In addition, many comments we get from alumni speak of the joy they feel at the comfortable way we work together. Our collaboration seems to have become an important part of the workshops, and completely unintended. And miracle of miracles, Suzanne has no interest whatsoever in becoming an actress.

An Improvised Life

CONTENTS

PROLOGUE

Some years ago I did a film with Madeline Kahn. A lot of it was shot on location, and one day we found ourselves at a particularly beautiful spot overlooking a panoramic view of the Hudson Valley. During a lull in the shooting, while the cameras were setting up, we went out onto an extensive lawn and sat there for a while, lost in the scenery. While we were musing and chatting, I found myself thinking about Madeline's many gifts. She was a fine actress, an excellent pianist; she had an exquisite operatic voice with impeccable technique and she was also a brilliant comedian. I asked her which of her talents she considered to be her primary focus. She thought for a while and couldn't come up with an answer. I don't think she'd ever thought about it before. "Well, what did you start out wanting to do?" I asked. "What was your first impulse? Was it acting?" She shook her head "no," but she didn't seem sure.

"Singing?"

"No."

"Playing the piano?"

"No."

"Did you want to be a comedian?"

"No, not really."

"Well, what was the first thing you thought of doing? There had to be something."

Again she tried to thread her way back to her childhood ambitions. "I used to listen to a lot of music." She paused, trying to find the words for what she was thinking. "And that's what I wanted to be," she finally said.

"I don't know what you mean," I said.

She answered, and it sounded as if she'd never formulated this thought before, as if it was news to herself.

"I wanted to be the music," she said.

It was a revelatory and somewhat disturbing moment. With that one statement I realized that what she'd said about herself was the impulse behind all of my own interests, all of my needs, all of my studying, compulsions, and passions, and had I been aware of that idea when I was starting out, had I been able to assimilate it, live within it, I would have saved endless years of frustration and work and confusion because that thought was at the very bottom of what I was looking for. So much had been invested in craft, in externalization, in looking for something solid out there that would fill the void, create a sense of flight, of getting out of the oppression of self.

We don't want to *do* it; we want to *be* it. Only we don't know it. No one tells us.

This is dedicated to everyone who wants to be the music.

PART
one

CHAPTER ONE

My father said that at the age of five I asked him if he could keep a secret. He said yes he could, so I told him I was going to be an actor when I grew up. At five, acting was already a fever in my blood, and somehow I knew, even then, that the decision was made and there would be no turning back. My father took my declaration with a grain of salt, knowing that children change their minds a dozen times before committing to something. I never changed my mind. My father had dreams of being a painter and a poet; and living with the ache of not having achieved his dreams he was keenly aware of the pitfalls involved in trying to have a career in the arts, so he mostly hoped I'd grow out of the idea. But my fate had been sealed before I had any notion of what I was letting myself in for, and my father bit his tongue.

Every film I saw, every play, every piece of music fed an unquenchable need to turn myself into something other than what I was. An aunt took me to see the ballet *Petrouchka*, and for months I became Stravinsky's marionette. I played the music on the phonograph over and over again, dancing every part. I was Petrouchka, the bears, the jugglers, the moor, my fantasy life so intense that I sometimes literally gave myself a fever in the process. The next year I was Louis Hayward in the film *The Man in the Iron Mask*, fighting, swaggering, swashbuckling, and finally escaping torture at the hands of my evil twin brother. The following year I became Charlie Chaplin. I remember having a temper tantrum when I wasn't allowed to sit through *The Great Dictator* for the third time, throwing myself on the floor of the movie theater, screaming bloody murder, and creating an embarrassing scene until my babysitter relented and sat back down, a hostage to my obsession. For months I tried to walk like Chaplin. I spent hours in front of a mirror pursing my mouth to the side, trying desperately to smile with that horizontal crease he had in his upper lip. I put on roller skates and swooped precariously on the edge of things. I performed endless imitations of Hitler through the filter of Chaplin's genius. Then, the following year, I became Danny Kaye, spending hour after hour in front of a mirror trying in vain to make my eyes turn down at the corners. I threw water on my hair to try and make it shake like his. I tried to scat-sing as fast as he could. Away from the mirror, I imitated anyone and everyone. Outside in the street, if I'd see someone with an interesting walk, in half an hour I'd made it my own. Any exotic behavior was fair game: a limp, an accent, a nervous tic, anything to turn myself into someone other than me. One day I was playing in the backyard with my cousins and my aunt overheard me say, "Let's play circus. I'll be everything."

I grew up in Brooklyn, and every Saturday afternoon, for years, I would drag my reluctant mother to acting classes at the Academy of Music, making her sit in dark, empty hallways while I studied whatever children worked on in those days. I was incorrigible. By age seven or eight I was completely obsessed with performing. Theater, movies, music—I was obsessed by all of them. At school my main activity was staring out the window and daydreaming about being other people in other times, other places. How I got through even grammar school remains a mystery.

I have two important memories from those early years. Both were small events, really, and neither took place in school. But both changed how I thought about theater and acting.

The first occurred when I went to a film with my father. I was around eight years old, but he took me to a movie for grown-ups, in black and white, with a lot of adult talk and not much action. In one scene a couple of actors were in a living room engaged in an intimate, intense dialogue about something or other, and I watched for a while, trying hard to keep up with their situation, which was too sophisticated for me. It was rare that anything on a movie screen ever bored me, but this was starting to do the trick, so to keep myself entertained I pretended I was there with them watching the scene from inside a closet. Where the impulse came from I don't know, but I held a hand up to my face and made a small opening in my fist so I could watch everything through the keyhole of an imaginary door. All of a sudden the acting, which had seemed real enough a moment ago, looked false, and the scene turned stale and lifeless. I was amazed. It was as though a veil had been lifted from my eyes. In an instant, the actors were no longer cinema gods with huge heads, the idols I had been imitating for years. They'd lost their sense of authority and importance. In fact, at this moment they no longer existed in any reality at all. The scene had instantly turned false, and I had the distinct feeling that the performances of the two people in the scene were no longer directed at each other but toward some anonymous audience. "But who is their audience?" I wondered. "There's no one in the room with them. They don't know I'm here, in the closet. They don't know anyone is watching. Who are they focusing on? Not me. Not any other living soul."

I immediately felt that it would have been more appropriate for them to be focusing on each other, which is what people did in real life, when no one was watching. But they weren't doing that. They were talking to no one and for no purpose.

This strange moment for me was simultaneously disillusioning and enlightening. It had come from a simple childhood trick, but it completely changed my view of acting, and for the first time gave me a perspective and a value system by which to gauge a performance. It was also the beginning of a kind of method for me, and its validity sustained me for about a decade. At least while watching other people's work. Gauging the truth of my own work was something that had to come later.

The second experience happened in the living room of our apartment. I was playing on the floor while my mother was consoling a friend who was in the middle of some kind of personal crisis. My mother listened patiently while the woman sat there crying her eyes out. I was halfway across the room, now pretending to read a book, but of course I was much more engrossed in the drama being played out in front of me. I watched the woman pouring her heart out to my mother and found myself slightly revolted. "I'm not moved by her performance," I thought. "What is she doing wrong?" I examined her clinically as she tried to get her story out through her pain and tears, and I finally came to the conclusion that I wasn't moved by her situation because she was crying too much. If she wanted to interest me, I thought, she'd better cut back on the tears a little and leave some room for me and my feelings. Of course, what I was watching was not a performance; this was real life. But life, even at age eight, was merely food for my obsession with acting. For me, theater was more important than life, more educational than life, and certainly more moving than life.

As I look back, I think what irked me about the woman's outpouring was that it was filled with self-pity, not an attractive quality on or off stage. Had I been more emotionally engaged at the time, or perhaps a few years older, I might have realized this, but I was too deeply into "all the world's a stage," so I was precocious in one way, not so much in another.

Many years later, at a time when I had become more connected to my own emotional life, I had an experience with an actress that gave me my first warning of what the craft of acting could do to people if they weren't careful. I was working on a television show that was not going well, and a couple of weeks in I was informed that one of the actors had been fired. This actor was loved by the whole cast, and for some reason it became my job to inform the other actors in the company.

The first person I told was a regular on the show, a woman I had worked with for some time. She was a fine actress and a lovely person. "I have bad news," I said to her, as gently as I could, trying to brace her. "So and so's been fired." The woman's jaw fell open and she froze for a few seconds while she kept looking at me. Then she said, "Can you see the look on my face?" She pointed to her face and held the expression. I knew immediately what she was doing. She'd had a spontaneous reaction, but it was too good to just feel and let go, so she was taking note and filing it away for future reference. It might be useful later on, in some performance. She wanted me to notice it, too. I could see her checking my reaction to her now-frozen expression, paying careful attention to how much I was moved by it, which would let her know if the look was effective.

I fell into immediate despair. Not just for her, but for myself too, because I had done the same thing on countless occasions. It is a habit that now fills me with revulsion—a habit perhaps valuable for the actor, and for his craft, but not so good for the human being living inside.

———————

From my earliest memory I had the strong sense that every character trait, every emotional condition possessed by the personalities I saw on screen, was accessible to me. In some deep place I always believed that what anyone else was feeling or doing, whether it be an act of heroism or cowardice or compassion or greed or villainy or anything in between, whatever the characters were going through emotionally was possible for me. I sensed that the entire range of emotions possessed by one human being was universal and available to everyone. Each of us had our own emphases and proclivities, but I intuitively believed that all of us were possessed of the entire spectrum of human feelings, and nothing that I've seen or felt since has convinced me otherwise.

Further, I had an instinct, even in those early days, that art was the direct injection of the artist's experiences into the audience, and that this transfusion was the highest purpose of all the arts. I felt that the epiphanies I'd had as a result of seeing other people's work, of exposure to other people's imaginations, whether through their acting or music or literature or painting, is what made the artists' experiences my own. I knew that these emotional adventures, transmitted from other people's triumphs or failures, were as real and tangible to me as a mathematical equation or a physics experiment. The artists' mastery of their craft gave them an invisible hypodermic injection that when inserted into me made me more than what I was. I could feel their essence working in my blood, and I knew myself to be capable of all manner of great and courageous things as a result of the art I'd been exposed to. The problem with these feelings, induced through the art of others, was that as real as they were, they didn't last. As I'd put down the book I was reading, or come out of the theater with my heart pounding and my imagination racing, there was no question that I could perform the same acts of transcendent courage or self-sacrifice that I saw and felt performed by the heroes whose lives I had become enmeshed in. But as the day wore on and my own daily activities and relationships came back into focus, the images and feelings inspired by whatever art form had riveted me would fade away and I'd be faced with my own fears and my own inadequacies. It was a deeply frustrating problem and one that I struggled with for years. What I realize now is that this is a good and healthy problem because it forces us, if we take the arts seriously, to constantly pit our own range of emotions and abilities against those behaviors that we can now feel are possible if we work on ourselves with patience and diligence.

At that time in my life I was unaware that I had any materials within me to work on. I had no sense that I myself was a work in progress, and that I was as malleable and formable as any character in a book or any piece of music or theatrical performance that I'd ever witnessed. It was an idea that had to wait many years for me to encounter consciously, and then many more years to embrace and work on. In short, at a very young age I'd become an addict. A film junkie. With all the dangers found in any other type of addiction. And like many addictions it pointed the way to something real and beautiful, but it also ran the risk of ruining my life.

CHAPTER TWO

My uncle Sandy was a fighter pilot during World War II. He flew a P-38, and between combat missions he wrote letters to my father saying, "If I make it through this war alive I'm going to buy a car and we're all going to move to California." Sandy made it through the war alive, came home with a chest full of medals, and immediately went out and bought a car.

I don't remember any of the arrangements, how we got past my parents quitting their jobs, what happened with the furniture and all our belongings, how they found a place to move to, the many good-byes, all of which were a blur for me, but in what seemed like just days I found myself squashed in the back seat of a sedan with my mother and brother, Sandy up front driving, my dad acting as co-pilot, and all of us heading to a new life in California. Through another uncle, who had written songs for several major films, my father had an introduction to someone in one of the film studios who could possibly help him to get work as a scene painter.

Consistent with a lot of my father's luck, the job didn't pan out. The week we arrived in Los Angeles a strike was called in the studios that lasted six months, and my father's first and only opportunity in the movie business dried up, but I was in heaven. We were in L.A. The golden land. The place where all my dreams would come true. We were in the movie capital of the world and I knew I'd be discovered within ten minutes of arriving.

Our first home was in the hills directly above Hollywood Boulevard, and every day after school I'd hike down to that magic street in the hopes that something major and life-changing would happen to me. Once I saw Sidney Toler, the actor who'd played Charlie Chan, and another time I passed Charlie Ruggles striding briskly down the boulevard, dressed to the teeth. Other than knowing they were professionals, I barely knew who they were, and I wasn't a fan of either actor, but seeing them in person, two honest-to-God, real-life movie stars, walking down the street just like ordinary people, thrilled me more than if I'd seen the president of the United States. There they were in three dimensions, real and tangible people. Their heads were no larger than mine, no matter how big they'd seemed in the movie theaters. It gave me hope.

I enrolled in junior high and found that miraculously there was a course called *acting* in the curriculum. It was taught by a warm, wonderful woman named Mrs. Lewis, who enjoyed her students and loved the process of putting on plays. We felt safe with her, and we all took chances, and had a terrific time. I felt nurtured and cared for and appreciated in school for perhaps the first time in my life. Her class was virtually the only thing I remember from junior high.

In high school things weren't as promising. The drama teacher was a failed actor with a lantern jaw and long grey hair. He looked like a cliché from a third-rate Shakespearean touring company, which is exactly what he'd been. His primary activity was telling us endless stories of his triumphs in little theaters around the country. Back then, we were properly impressed. The one comment I can remember his making about my work, probably casual on his part, seared me like a branding iron. "You might end up being a comedian," he said, "but you'll never be an actor." His remark was tossed off, something he probably forgot the minute he said it, but now fifty years later it still lives with me. Without his help or encouragement I auditioned for all the school plays and got leads in every one. There was also a course in radio broadcasting taught by a wonderful woman named Lucy Assadorian. She was a tiny, immaculately dressed, beautiful woman who was worshipped by every boy in the class. With her encouragement, along with the radio plays we put on in her class and the stage plays I was cast in, I managed to survive high school.

Throughout the entire four years, I don't believe I ever opened a work of nonfiction. I cut every possible class to hang out in the theater, forging the names of teachers and my parents whenever I had to. The teachers used to say to me on a regular basis, "Alan, you could do *so much* for this school if you put your mind to it." I didn't want to put my mind to it. I didn't want to do anything for the school. It wasn't doing much for me and I thought it only fair to reciprocate. How I graduated remains a mystery.

Chorus was of some interest to me. So was a class in ceramics run by a Miss Beatty, a wonderfully imaginative, eccentric, and completely unappreciated woman who at one point literally chased me around her studio with a glaze pot in an attempt to have me at least *try* to work with the stuff. I refused. All of my ceramics remained rough terra cotta. I also remember one history teacher, Mr. Engles, a thoroughly decent man with a passion for history so great that he allowed us to approach the subject from any vantage point that made sense to us, and in any form that we could identify with. In his classroom I wrote my first play. It was on the topic of slavery in the United States. I think I got an *A*. Probably the only grade above a *C* I received in my four years there.

High school consistently made me feel as if I were in prison, but being in plays sustained me. I lived for the rehearsals and performances. It was the only arena in which I felt that I had any identity and any purpose. As I write this it seems strange to think that for so many years my sense of comfort and identity was secured only when I was being someone else, but I think this is true of many actors.

My own unformed personality found grounding and shape in the words and actions of the characters in the scripts, and I would turn into the characters during rehearsals and stay within them until long after the plays had finished their runs.

It was around this time that I began to study guitar. Like most of my hobbies, playing the guitar began as an attempt to keep my mind off acting, and gave me something to occupy my mind when I didn't have a part in a play. I worked hard at the guitar, and soon got good enough to perform at functions around L.A. I masqueraded as a folk singer, but I was a maverick within the folk scene because folk music wasn't a particular passion of mine. I was more interested in jazz, but wasn't disciplined enough to learn jazz guitar.

At that time there was a singer who'd become very popular in folk circles, a big, impressive black woman with a huge voice and commanding presence who wowed audiences throughout Los Angeles. We'd often be on the same bill together and I was never comfortable listening to her. I could never understand her success. She sang the music of her people, spirituals and blues, and some gospel, but what she was doing never worked for me. There was something about her that I found annoying, and I couldn't figure out what it was until a couple of years later when I heard Mahalia Jackson and it all clicked. This woman on the folk circuit was singing the pain of her people, the pain of being black, the pain of her life, and I suppose she struck the same false note in me that was struck by my mother's friend in the living room, when I was eight. Mahalia Jackson on the other hand made me cry. "What was the difference between this woman on the circuit and Mahalia Jackson?" I asked myself, and I struggled with this question for weeks until I finally realized that Mahalia Jackson's singing was a joyful *release* from the pain of her life. Her pain and suffering were present in her singing, there was no way for her to escape; in every note she sang it was clear that she'd had a huge burden to carry, but she was singing to rise above it. Singing to liberate herself from her pain and to share the joy of the music with anyone who cared to listen. The woman on the folk circuit was simply singing her pain. In doing so she was inflicting it on me, making me feel as if I owed her something, and that it was somehow my job to alleviate her suffering. I wanted to be like Mahalia Jackson.

In those days I thought that my feelings about other people's performances were objective. I felt there was a component to an actor's work that went beyond taste and personal preference. I still feel that way in part, although I also recognize that there is a time when people are ready for certain emotional experiences and not for others. There have been times in my life when I've dismissed certain works of art as being stupid or boring, only to find a couple of decades later that I was not mature enough at the time to appreciate them. It's hard to admit we don't understand something. I am still amazed, for example, at someone's being afraid of Beethoven. I've known people who can't listen to his music because it's too emotionally arousing or overwhelming for them. But for me, Beethoven's music was for decades almost as crucial as eating or drinking. His work was a prod into a life of courage, a life embraced totally with all its pain and all its challenges, and for many years I felt that I almost couldn't live without his music. Had I been afraid of what Beethoven's music evoked in me I think that fact alone would have given me reason to listen to it, to try and decipher my fears and attempt to understand and get beyond them.

Around this time, while I was still in high school, I went to see a film that had won its star an Academy Award. The work was a theater classic, translated into a film for the star, and like millions of other people I came out of the theater enormously impressed by his performance. But along with being impressed, I left the theater also feeling jealous and inept, and then hating myself for those feelings, and then hating the actor for piling on more feelings of inadequacy and depression. "What the hell was wrong with me?" I wondered. "Why couldn't I simply enjoy the man's work?" Here was obviously a great actor doing the part of his life, giving a performance that had gotten him enormous attention, awards, accolades, and all I could do was grouse about it and hate him for it. I stayed feeling depressed and inadequate for days.

A month later I saw Walter Huston in *The Devil and Daniel Webster*. This time I left the theater walking on air, filled with a sense of delight and joy and possibility. I stopped in my tracks. "What was the difference?" Two performances, seen weeks apart, both considered great. One fills me with gloom, jealousy, and despair; the other makes me feel alive and buoyant.

I thought about it for weeks. I compared the two actors endlessly and finally came up with this realization. In the first instance, the actor who'd won the Academy Award was trying to impress me. He was demonstrating how beautifully he spoke, how well he articulated the lines, how beautifully he phrased them, how rich was the musical tone in his voice, how well he moved. And what I came to realize was that in spite of all the attention he received, the audiences had not been given a genuine experience. They were applauding their own intelligence at recognizing the actor's technical prowess. The actor was congratulating himself, and the audiences were also congratulating themselves. But in his performance I couldn't find that injection of experience that I needed so badly, that hypodermic connection that bonded me to the actor and would make his experience mine. I wasn't allowed to *be* the character, and I started to wonder whether anyone had actually been affected by his work or whether that sense of narcissism was all anyone wanted from an actor. It slightly revolted me. I finally decided that his Academy Award had been given as an act of self-congratulation by the Academy, people applauding their own perceptions. Walter Huston on the other hand presented me with the gift of a whole person, fully articulated and realized, un-self-conscious and completely filled with his own joy at doing the work. I wanted to be like Walter Huston.

CHAPTER THREE

All of my performances in the plays throughout high school were successful. I got laughs, I got applause, I got very good comments after the shows, and in this one arena I started to have some small stature in a school completely dominated by its athletic program. But after each performance—no matter how well my work seemed to go, no matter how much applause or how many laughs, no matter how well I was able to manipulate the audience into feeling things and focusing on me—afterward, in the dressing room, I would inevitably feel depressed. Cheated out of something. I didn't know what it was until in my senior year of high school, when I began studying with Benjamin Zemach.

Benjamin taught small classes in Hollywood, a two-hour streetcar ride from where we had moved to in Highland Park. Benjamin was a tiny giant of a man who lived and breathed theater, and his classes were warm and supportive and serious. He had studied with Stanislavski, and I heard from someone that his personality was very similar to Stanislavski's. Benjamin possessed a fierce focus and a burning devotion to conveying truth onstage. I don't remember how I found my way to his classes; they were small and for the most part not attended by aspiring professionals, but he treated his students with great respect and he demanded a lot from them. When I started to work with him I expected that I would get singled out and praised. I felt comfortable and at ease on the stage; I knew my work had humor, that I could command attention.

It didn't happen. He was unimpressed. I'd do a scene and expect laughter, applause, a nod, some kind of recognition that I was a thinking actor and knew my way around the stage. Instead I found myself ignored. It began eating at me. We began scene study, and scene after scene he remained disapproving. At one point he said to me, "Where are you coming from?"

"What do mean?" I answered.

"Where did you come from just then?"

"I came from offstage," I said. Where else would I be coming from?

"That's what's wrong," he said. "Your character has no past. I see an actor walking onto a stage. I don't see a human being coming in from the cold outdoors. Coming home from a job that is a disappointment to him. Coming back to a family that only partially nourishes him."

It took some time for his words to sink in, many months, but slowly it became clear to me that there was more to acting than being clever and being able to get a lot of attention, and that in spite of the lip service I'd been paying to creating life onstage, in spite of my intense examination of other actors' performances and the lives of people around me, my own work had no real reference to that truth and that reality. I began to realize that the depression I'd consistently felt after my own performances was an unconscious signal that I had been telling lies onstage, that my work was shallow and manipulative. Benjamin never actually said it, but I could tell that this criticism was behind his silence. I began analyzing my own performances, using Benjamin's eyes and ears, and I came up short month after month. I started to write long biographies of the characters I was playing, hoping to please him, to get some sense from him that I was on the right track. Nothing worked. The biographies of my characters got longer, my research got more and more extensive, and my temper grew worse. Something was not happening. I didn't know what it was; I didn't know why I was so miserable, so unable to get even a smile from him, a nod, some sense of encouragement.

Then, one day, after working with Benjamin for about a year and a half, during the first performance of a play we'd been rehearsing, something happened. I had done the research, the endless biographical work, the meticulous thinking, obsessing about the part day and night, and probably because of this—my sweat, my devotion, my need—a small miracle took place. I was playing the part of a soldier returning home from a war, coming back to his wife and family after having been wounded on the front. I was about eighteen at the time and had never been anywhere near a war, nor did I have the vaguest idea of how to be a husband or a father. But when I walked onto that stage I became the character. No, that's the wrong way of describing it. When I walked onto the stage it was as if the character told me to get out of the way and mind my own business. The character took on a life of his own, with an immediacy and a purpose that had little to do with any of the preparation I had done. My voice changed. My posture changed. The line readings that I'd become used to went out the window, my timing became different, and my relationships onstage with the other actors were more real than anything in my own life. The woman playing my wife was truly my own beloved wife; I understood her better than I understood myself. And the war I was returning from was real, and oppressive, and frightening. And more importantly, these details all took care of themselves in one sweep, without my attending to any of them. For years afterward I described this event by saying, "It was as if I were outside of my body, watching the play from perhaps forty feet above the stage. I could see the entire event playing below, and I was gleefully calling out to the part of me that was on the stage doing the play: 'Go! Go! Keep it up!'" The experience lasted perhaps twenty minutes, but it changed my life forever. For those few minutes I was living in a state of grace. It was a place where nothing could go wrong. There was no possibility of criticism, of evaluation, of discussion, because I was simply witnessing an event. It was the most important, the most significant and wonderful moment of my life, and I was barely present to experience it.

Benjamin beamed at me afterward and his approval was warming, but oddly not crucial. The experience had a depth and reality to it that went past any need for approval from him or anyone. And as much as I had loved, *needed* acting before that event, from that moment on I became an acting junkie. I now lived not just for acting, for being in front of an audience, but for the possibility of that exalted experience returning. I lived for those moments when the part played me and I was completely out of the way. These moments began happening with some frequency because of the fervor with which I attacked each part, but there was no knowing when they would happen or for how long. I found that I could do the work leading up to these moments, but I could not summon them at will.

At this point I began to feel that when one of these events was *not* taking place I was cheating the audience. When I found myself present, when the character refused to take me over, when I was acting with technique and no inspiration, I became embarrassed to be in front of the audience, and I'd steal away from the theater as if I were a thief. But no matter how hard I worked, I couldn't control when these experiences would take hold of me.

Years later I began to see that others shared this experience of flow, of knowing things they had no way of knowing, of being witness to events from some high vantage point when the "self" is completely out of the way and they are flying somehow, and another part of them, a better part of them, is the vehicle.

It is when you *are* the music.

Athletes experience it; they call it being in the zone. They say that when it happens time slows down. They know the positions of each player on the field, they can't miss the ball, and they can't make mistakes.

Doctors can have it; they too can be in the zone. I've heard doctors say on occasion, "Yes, there have been times when a patient comes in and I'll immediately know what they're suffering from. Sometimes it will be an illness I've barely heard of, or never dealt with, but I know what they've got and how to treat it."

Teacher's can have this experience, too. I've heard them say, "I knew there was something going on with Tommy at home. He said nothing about it, I didn't even particularly see a change in him, but something told me there was a problem, and I knew instinctively what it was."

As time went on I became aware that people in all walks of life have this experience, with this in common: that it only seems to take place with those who are deeply devoted to the art or sport or work in which it is occurring.

In the early days, when these experiences happened to me, I was so engrossed in acting that I didn't take the time to explore the other arenas in which these "zone" experiences grabbed hold of people's lives, so in my naïveté I allowed it to be a magical property, belonging only to the craft of acting. I worshipped at the altar of my profession, and as a result made an interesting mistake. What I allowed myself to believe was that the craft of acting had given me a great gift—that there was a magical aspect inherent in my craft and in no other, that I had tapped into it and that this magic made the craft of acting worthy of worship. What I didn't realize at the time was that there is nothing special whatsoever in the craft of acting. Acting can be anything one wants it to be, from the most crass, dead, ego-driven activity, used as a way of earning an easy living or finding women, on the one end, to something sublime, magical, and transforming on the other. And the difference, the only difference, is the investment made by the person who's engaged in the process. In other words, it wasn't a gift that the craft of acting had bestowed on me, it was a gift that I had bestowed on the craft of acting. My diligence and devotion allowed me to experience this wonderful and transforming place.

One of the saddest things I've ever heard anyone say was at a dinner party a few years ago. A friend of mine was there, he's a pretty decent musician and composer, and I found myself talking about this place, this "zone," which was for me as close to having a direct connection to the universe as I could imagine, and I asked him if he'd ever experienced being in that place. He said yes, that a few times while playing Bach in symphony orchestras he'd felt that sense of being played by the music, as if Bach were in control and not he. Then he went on to say that it was the most frightening experience he'd ever had, and hoped it would never happen again. I felt terribly sorry for my friend, for his fear of losing control, and for his anxiety that without a tight rein on himself he would fly off into some dangerous and unknown place. I suppose for some people it is a risk, but I would not want to live without having the possibility of these flights in my life. They remain the best places I have ever been. The only real change that has taken place in me, in regard to these magical experiences, is that through the years I have come to worship the place itself and not the craft that has brought me to it. But I'm getting ahead of myself.

One night in class, Benjamin told us of a production he'd seen in Moscow, decades earlier, perhaps it was in the 1920s, a production of the opera *Prince Igor*. He described a scene in which the Czar was sitting on his throne in the middle of the stage. At some point, into the scene trooped an enormous crowd of peasants who were being allowed a rare audience with their Czar. In Russia, in those days, the productions were often enormous, and Benjamin estimated that the extras numbered a hundred, perhaps even more. Benjamin went on to describe a moment when the Czar imperiously looked around the stage and caught the eye of one of the peasants. The peasants had been instructed to look down, not to dare look the Czar in the face. But this one serf raised his eyes and looked directly at the monarch. For a peasant to be even in the presence of the Czar was a miracle, a life-transforming experience. But to have locked eyes with the Czar? Unthinkable! Benjamin mimed the moment as he spoke. As he related the story, he demonstrated the expression on the Czar's face—regal, haughty, and superior—and then he showed us the look on the face of the peasant. At first the peasant's look was one of shock and wonder. He was being looked on by the Czar! Fear crept into his eyes. Would he be able to survive this experience? It was almost too much for him to take in. He was staring into the sun. And then when the Czar broke his gaze from the peasant and looked away, the peasant turned slowly toward the audience and his face showed a mixture of awe, wonder, and joy past all imagining, as if he had seen the face of God. And we could see from Benjamin's imitation of the peasant, the look on his face, that the peasant's life was transformed for all time.

When Benjamin finished telling us the story we sat silently for a while, silent and enthralled. Afterward, on the trip home I thought about what had happened. This moment, this tiny moment in the play, so moving to Benjamin when he had seen it some forty years earlier, had now deeply affected a group of acting students six thousand miles and two generations away from where it had taken place—the work of an extra in a huge production riddled with extras. It had been a passing moment in a play about something else. It had lasted perhaps fifteen seconds of stage time. Not one word had been spoken and yet the work of this extra had crossed seas, mountains, countries, languages, and decades, to be shared by us in an acting class and moving us as deeply as if it had just happened.

I have rarely had such a sense of the power of this strange profession I am in.

CHAPTER FOUR

One day, sometime in 1954, out of nowhere I received a long-distance call from John Bennes. The year before, he and I had been in a terrible production of *The Merchant of Venice*. We became friends and then he disappeared off the face of the Earth.

"Where the hell are you?" I yelled over the phone.

"Vermont," he said.

"Why?" I asked.

"I got a scholarship to Bennington College here."

"Isn't that a girls' school?" I asked.

"Yes, it is."

"Well done!" I said.

"You want to come? I can recommend you."

"What do I have to do?"

"Just show up. I can get you an interview with the guy who does the interviews."

"How did you get a scholarship to a girls' school, or should I ask?" I said.

"They keep four guys on campus to act in the plays. You can take classes, get credits, and graduate. Among other things," he replied.

"I'm broke," I said. "What's it going to cost me?"

"Zip," John replied. "You get room, board, tuition, and maid service."

"I'm on my way," I said.

With a change of clothes, a loaf of bread, half a pound of cheese, and a salami, I said some good-byes, put my entire savings—all twenty dollars of it—in my jeans, and started hitch-hiking to Vermont. When I got hungry I stopped at railroad trestles, cut up some cheese, salami, and bread with a pocket knife, and stared down at the tracks. If it rained, I'd find a car, crawl under it, and take a nap. At the time it all felt very romantic and European. I look back at it now with my heart in my mouth.

It took about a week to get to Bennington. By the time I arrived, my friend Bennes had left. I think he got a job in a play somewhere but I never found out. Once on campus, I brushed the road off my leather jacket, walked into the administration office, and told them my business. To my relief I learned that my interview was still on the schedule. They directed me to the home of Howard Nemerov, who was the head of the English Department and soon to be poet laureate of the United States. The news didn't make me particularly comfortable; this was starting to feel way out of my league. I walked to Nemerov's home, wandering past pristine New England cottages that comprised most of the campus, feeling like an extra in a Judy Garland movie. I found the place and knocked on the door. Nemerov opened it, invited me in, sat me down, and proceeded to question me about theater, film, and literature while immediately plying me with numerous martinis, the first I'd ever had. To my delight, they made me very happy and reasonably articulate. They seemed to have the same effect on him. The professor and I proceeded to get plastered together, and got along famously. So famously, in fact, that he accepted me into the college without even bothering to ask for my Los Angeles City College transcripts, which, fortunately for me, had not yet arrived. The transcripts didn't get to Bennington for another two weeks. Once they did come, they were read by the admissions people with considerable dismay, but it was too late to get rid of me. I was Nemerov's guy. The professor and I were old drinking buddies by then, and the die had been cast. Through a series of accidents and miracles, I was now one of the drama guys.

I was happy to leave L.A. City College. I didn't like the kind of work they were doing there. It felt stagy and artificial. The actors were all pre-Brando types, talking at the tops of their lungs, trying to impress each other, and mostly demonstrating their talents in the hallways rather than on the stage. The professors were people who hadn't made it in the profession and were busy using the students as their captive audience, posturing and enunciating as if their lives depended on it. Our job was to applaud their performances. I had turned sullen and incommunicative, and didn't fit in at all. There or anywhere else for that matter. A friend of mine who'd been with me at L.A. City College told me that years later, after I'd had some success, it was said about me, "We didn't understand him then, and we don't understand him now." Their reaction delighted me to no end.

At Bennington there were plenty of sullen, maladjusted types like me, and I fit right in. Also, there were martinis galore, whenever I stretched out my arm. It was a glorious two years and would have made a good premise for a sit-com. I met a lot of rich co-eds, did a lot of acting, and drank a lot of martinis. My parents were going through a very difficult financial time, and to cover my expenses they sent me, believe it or not, a dollar a month, which, at the time—with room, food, and tuition all covered by the school—was all I seemed to need.

There were two professors in the drama department, and both of them had a profound effect on me, but for very different reasons. One was Larry Arrick, an intense, brilliant, young aspiring director who pushed me further along in the direction that Benjamin had been taking me. The other, after directing me as Bill Walker in a production of *Major Barbara*, criticized my work by saying it was too improvisational. He wanted me to pin down the part precisely, without any variations. He gave me a poor grade on the performance, and his assessment really annoyed me. I had worked hard on the part, and felt happy with what I was doing. He had no problem with my core interpretation of the role, and admitted that the central idea remained consistent from performance to performance. His criticism was related to embellishments that I needed to change each night, depending on what was taking place at the moment. I told him that this was the way I wanted to play the part, that my choices were intentional, and this was the way I wanted to approach my work.

The professor didn't have any interest in my approach or my needs, and his disapproval became a turning point for me. I had always been good about taking criticism from directors, but not this time. This man was so far from understanding what I was about that he actually helped me define what kind of an actor I wanted to be—needed to be. The thought of doing something exactly the same way, over and over again, felt like the death of any kind of creativity. I didn't know where my work was headed, but I knew that it couldn't be where this teacher was pointing.

The scholarship lasted a couple of years, during which time I tried to apply myself to academic work, but it was too late. My inadequate skills at writing papers, even of thinking linearly, caught up with me, and I either quit or got kicked out depending on who you talk to. It was probably a combination of both. What didn't help matters was that on the spur of the moment I had married a music and dance student at the college, Jeremy Yaffe. She was eighteen, I was twenty-one; the school was not pleased. We left the college and headed to New York without a thought in our heads of what would happen next. Within a couple of weeks, we found out that Jeremy was pregnant.

Floundering in New York with a pregnant wife to care for, I tried looking for acting work to no avail. I wanted desperately to be responsible. I even attempted a few real jobs, the kinds of jobs grown-ups do, but I couldn't do them. I remember one that consisted of sitting in a dimly lit room with a large herd of people—a set designed by Terry Gilliam—a nightmare place with automatons sitting silently at desks, checking numbers written on endless small slips of paper. I sat there for about three hours, checking my numbers, warding off a panic attack, but finally breaking into a cold sweat. I took off my jacket, loosened my tie, then went to the overseer and told him I had to go to the bathroom. He said okay, and I ran down about ten flights of stairs and never looked back, leaving an expensive sports jacket in my wake as well as a huge pile of unchecked numbers.

I couldn't do jobs. I was constitutionally unable to devote myself to anything outside the arts, pregnant wife or no pregnant wife. As a stopgap, just to pay for food, I connected with a group of young folk singers, with Erik Darling on banjo and Bob Carey on guitar. They were looking for an additional voice and I thought, "Why the hell not?" It would be a way of earning a few bucks on weekends, while looking for acting work. The group was called The Tarriers, from the Irish folksong "Drill Ye Tarriers, Drill." *Tarrier* means worker. We were often referred to as "The Terriers," but we didn't care much.

To our own immense surprise we started getting decent jobs, and quickly landed a recording contract. We put out a couple of hit songs, and for a couple of years I traveled with them around the United States and Canada, and through much of Europe. The money was good enough that Jeremy and our son Adam, who was now nearly one year old, could join me on most of our travels, Adam many nights sleeping in a hotel bathtub with a blanket for a lining. We were young; we'd never been to Europe before, and for a while it was a great adventure. And in my naïveté I thought singing in a successful group would be an entrée into the theater. But of course no such thing happened.

One day, after a whirlwind tour of Switzerland and Germany, we were in the middle of a show at the legendary Olympia theater in Paris. I looked down at myself with a guitar strapped around my neck, a checked shirt opened practically to the navel, black satin pants shining away, and I said, "What the hell is this? Who am I?" Everything felt strange and surreal. I missed acting. I missed having a home. After the show I told the other guys that I'd be leaving after the few weeks that remained of the tour.

The tour over, Jeremy, Adam, and I returned to the States and I went back to looking for acting work in New York. None came. After many months I was offered a job in an off-Broadway play. I was hired because they needed a lute player. I'd never seen a lute in my life, but it had six strings, like a guitar, which I thought was close enough. I tuned it as best I could, sang an old English folk song to the director, and got the job. I had about six lines in the play and earned more money than anyone else in the cast because the musicians' union paid better than Actors' Equity. The cast's retribution was that I was shunned from all backstage conversations about acting, since I was a lowly musician. The play had a very good run, well over a year, at which point I put away my lute and tunic and went back to being an unemployed actor, now with a wife and son to look after.

Some months later I got a call from the husband of a friend of mine from Bennington. His name was David Shepherd and he was forming an improvisational group to play for the summer at the Crystal Palace in St. Louis. I auditioned for him, got a place in the troupe of four, moved Jeremy and Adam out to St. Louis, and spent a few months working professionally at my craft for the first time in my life. It was hard work because I wasn't initially adept at improvisation. I wasn't loose enough or facile enough.

Sometime during the summer, a man named Paul Sills came down from Chicago to see the group. One night, after the show, he approached me and said if I ever wanted a job in Chicago I should look him up. I thanked him profusely but inwardly said, "Fat chance. I'm not going to bury myself in Chicago for a hundred dollars a week. I'm going to have a career in New York."

In the middle of the summer Jeremy informed me she was pregnant again. We returned to New York, me once again without a job and with no prospects. Finally, the insecurity of our life became too much for Jeremy, and within months of the birth of our second son, Matthew, she took the children and left.

I held out in New York for another year, deeply missing my family, praying for something to present itself; nothing did. In a state of complete despair I called this man Sills to see if the job in Chicago was still available.

Making that call was like phoning in my own obituary. Taking this job would absolutely end my chances of doing anything major in either New York or Los Angeles. In no way did I think it could lead back to theater, or film. Chicago had no theatrical importance in those days; this felt like a death sentence for my career.

But another part of me said, "What have I got to lose? Nothing's happening here; I'm giving up a myth. At least I'll be working at my craft for the first time in my life. I'll be eating, and I'll be able to send money to Jeremy and help out with the kids."

I called Sills and said I was ready to come to Chicago if the job was still open. He said it was, so once again I packed up and headed out of town toward an uncertain future. The name of the hole-in-the-wall theater was Second City, and within six months we were getting national attention. That was fifty years ago, and Second City is still going strong.

———

The serious start of my professional life began with Second City. Everything up to that point was prelude and rehearsal. I threw myself into the work with a feverish passion. I lived in a ten-by-ten-foot room with a bathroom down the hall, ate at a hotel across the street, and did my laundry at a Laundromat a couple of blocks away, but I didn't even notice the conditions. I was ecstatic. I had a life. I had somewhere to go, a place to be responsible to on a daily basis, people to work with and get to know. I could be financially responsible for my children.

Often, after the show, my friend Sheldon Patinkin and I would go to the Clark Theater, which played art films and stayed open all night. We'd watch foreign films with religious, worshipful attention, and then afterward walk miles back to Old Town, tearing apart and analyzing every moment of what we'd seen. Sheldon was the general manager of Second City. We became friends one day when Bernie Sahlins, our producer, said he wanted to start a film series on Saturday afternoons. He said he needed a couple of volunteers to run it. I raised my hand; Sheldon raised his. Bernie told us to design a list of films for the series. I said to Sheldon, "Why don't you write down your favorite twenty films, I'll do the same, and we'll compare notes." Sheldon went off and wrote his list in about four minutes; I did too, and we compared. They were the same list. We became friends on the spot, and have remained friends to this day. And fifty years later, we still have the same lists!

To this day I'm not sure why Sills hired me. My work for the first several months wasn't good. I didn't know how to be funny on cue. I wasn't clever. My work often lapsed into the maudlin and overly serious. The other members of the company were more versed in the political and social issues of the day, and I started to become concerned that I wasn't going to make it there, which was a terrifying thought. If I couldn't make it at Second City, there was no place for me anywhere.

After several abortive and frustrating months, and a feeling of impending doom, I found a character who, although I took him seriously, managed to make the audience laugh. I hung on to this one character like a life preserver. For weeks he was my survival mechanism. He was the only character I would go near. Whatever my assignment, I'd do it as this one character. I suppose it wasn't surprising, since from the beginning I always thought of myself as a character actor—someone who transforms himself into other people. I had no interest in being myself onstage. In fact, there was no possibility of my playing myself on the stage because I didn't know who I was. I didn't have a clue. I only knew myself as other people, and this character that I found, whoever he was, became my anchor.

In the months that followed, as I became more comfortable and secure, I started to let go a little and I began to explore other characters. I found a proud and untrusting young Puerto Rican, a devil-may-care Italian worker, a stalwart and stoic old Jew—all of them immigrants or misfits. I felt at home as a foreigner. As a stranger. As anyone who was an ocean away from his own environment and a million miles away from his own identity, whatever that was. Interestingly, at that time I was aware only of the great variety of characters I was playing. The fact that they were all foreigners and misfits didn't occur to me until years later when I had started down a path of self-examination, and realized that this was the way I saw myself.

For all the intense work I had done within the craft, within the confines of the safe and comfortable box I called *acting*, I had done no work on the mystery of my own self. In fact I had no idea that work could be done on this self, or that help was available out there from endless sources and in hundreds of modalities. I was too busy enjoying the fruits of a quarter-century of preparation to notice that outside my life as an actor I had almost no life at all.

CHAPTER FIVE

Here's the way the shows at Second City worked. There was a formal part of the evening that lasted about forty-five minutes. Then there was an intermission, at the beginning of which the performers took suggestions from the audience. The second half of the show consisted of improvisations based on the suggestions given to us by the audience. These suggestions were in categories such as current events, people in the news, movie titles, book titles, song titles, and proverbs. During the twenty-minute intermission, the eight of us raced backstage to formulate the second half of the show, trying desperately to come up with material that might work. We'd pace, we'd think, we'd smoke, we'd sweat, we'd confer with each other in a desperate attempt to create viable material. Two-people relationship scenes, blackouts, pantomimes, the reworking of old jokes—every night was guerrilla warfare or a kamikaze raid. Before going onstage to perform the improv section of the show, we lived in a state of terror. Sometimes, on weekends, we did two shows a night, which meant we got to feel this terror twice. But what a gift it was! What a deep and concentrated training it was, and what a blessing. And the intensity of those shows! My God, we'd play ten, fifteen, sometimes twenty different characters during the course of an evening. Some ideas worked, some didn't; the ones that worked became part of a library of characters we'd hang on to and even use later on, after we'd moved away from improvisational theater and were acting in plays or movies, or even if we'd switched over to writing. But most importantly, the thing that separated my experience at Second City from every other endeavor I've ever been connected with was that we were in an arena where we were allowed to experiment. To change. To grow. And not only that, we were we allowed to fail. *Allowed to fail!* And audiences came to the theater knowing this was very likely to happen. They knew that part of every evening wasn't going to work. They came to Second City to see process unfold, and they knew that if one scene was terrible there was every possibility the next one would be memorable.

God help us, we are living in a civilization where *failure* is a dirty word. It's become a moral issue. If you fail at something you are a bad person. Failure doesn't look good on ledger sheets. You have to explain it to stockholders, and sadly this kind of thinking has permeated every nook and cranny of our civilization. We don't have the time anymore to learn from trial and error. We have to do everything right the first time, and continue to do it right ever after. But how in the world are we to grow if we don't fail? Is it possible to have an endless series of successes without falling on our faces? I suppose it is, but I think it would entail doing the same things over and over again without taking chances, without taking risks or exploring our limits, without finding out what we can and can't do. And if we don't grow, we decay. It's that simple. Nothing in our universe is static. There's no other possibility. At Second City we weren't allowed to decay. My gratitude for permission to fail, granted by our producer, Bernie Sahlins, and our director, Paul Sills, is endless. There are people who come up to me to this day and talk about improvisations they saw at the club almost fifty years ago, and in their faces you know that these memories were magical and have stayed completely alive.

One night, about six months into my life at Second City, I improvised a scene with one of the women in the company that got an enormous audience reaction. It was a relationship scene and it ran over fifteen minutes, which was much longer than most of the material being done at the club at that time. With Sills directing, we rehearsed it for the next few days, fine-tuned it, and put it into the show. It was perhaps the best work I'd ever done, and certainly one of the best things my partner had ever done. Around that time the club was approached by some producers who wanted us to do an hour-long special for Canadian television. This would be a huge break for many reasons, not least of which was that it would be the first time any of us had ever been on television. The special would be shot in our theater, with a live audience, and my new scene with this actress was to be one of the centerpieces of the show.

As the weeks went on and the TV special loomed closer, I began to feel that the actress I was working with was no longer relating to me. I felt she'd stopped listening to anything I said, and working with her started becoming unpleasant and difficult. The TV show was upon us, and once again I felt my career—my whole future—was at stake. As we continued to perform the scene in the club, I became more and more frustrated. During the scene every other word out of my mouth was "Listen!" and each night it became more emphatic. "*Listen!*" I'd say to her. "*Listen* to me!" I couldn't seem to make any impact; I couldn't get her to play ball or to bounce off me. Looking back at it now, I know that her behavior came out of fear. At the time it felt like selfishness, something that she was doing to upstage me and take all the attention for herself, and it drove me crazy. I became so annoyed with her and the way the scene was going that I started to miss laughs, my timing was thrown, and I even began to feel that the audience was starting to dislike me. They didn't seem to be concerned with my partner's selfishness; they didn't notice that she wasn't *listening* to me, one of the first lessons every actor is supposed to learn. In fact, the worse it got, the more I struggled, the more positive the audience's reaction to her seemed to be. I began to intensely dislike the audience, feeling betrayed by what I'd felt until then had been a very intelligent crowd, a *university* crowd. We had a *following*, for God's sake, people who came back, show after show, and up to now had demonstrated taste and intelligence. I started to hate them, and the actress too, and I began to dread doing the scene. Once again I felt my career slipping away.

I tried everything I could think of to fight my way back into the scene. I tried rethinking my character; I tried not paying any attention to the actress, both to regain my power on stage and to give her a dose of her own medicine. I tried to punch up my delivery, I tried talking louder, I tried interrupting her. Nothing worked. A day or so before the TV show, as a last resort, in desperation, hoping for any straw to hang on to, I found myself thinking, "I'm going to love her. Whatever she does, I'm going to accept her just the way she is—I'm going to love her." Where that idea came from, I will never know. It was completely out of character, completely unlike me. I had never before thought in those terms. At that point in my life the word *love* was not much in my vocabulary, but there you are, desperation does interesting things. I went onstage that evening with one thought in my mind, "I'm going to love her. Whatever she does, I'm going to love her," and the whole scene came back to me. The character came back, my laughs came back, the audience regained their intelligence, and I found some peace for the first time in weeks. It was probably the most important realization I had ever come to. At that time I didn't have the wisdom to realize that I had stumbled upon a crucial tool for life—it was simply a way to make the scene work, which was the deepest understanding I was capable of reaching. My work onstage seemed manageable, sometimes even understandable and concrete. Life offstage was an impenetrable mystery. I wish I'd had the sense then to realize that for a big life, a *macro* life, the walls between career and life have to come crashing down, but I had not yet reached that level of self-knowledge. It took another five years for that idea to begin penetrating my consciousness, and even then it came by microscopic increments. At the time I was still too much in the thrall of earning a living in the field I had been plowing for twenty-five years. There were still worlds to conquer.

For the next six months things got better and better. The group became tighter, we took endless chances, our repertoire grew broader, we had an intensely socially conscious base that we all shared, and we felt proud of our niche and thumbed our noses at "the commercial theater." I remember an evening when David Merrick came to the show. At that point Merrick practically owned Broadway. He showed up at Second City on a packed Friday night, without a reservation, announced his name, and the manager said, "Oh, hi. We have a full house but we can probably find a place for you to stand in the back." "I guess you didn't hear me," Merrick said imperiously. "My name is *David Merrick*." The manager said, "Oh! In that case we'll *definitely* find you a place to stand in the back." Merrick watched the show standing in the back. We all thought it was great.

I stayed with the group in Chicago for a year. I found out, very late in the year, that when I was hired it was intended that I front a second wave of actors, the second company; the first company had long been slated to go to New York. But I had gotten along so well with them that I was now asked to stay with the first company and join them in their Broadway debut. Needless to say, I was ecstatic.

From my one year in Chicago I gained ten years worth of experience. We all did. We did every kind of scene imaginable. We played characters of all ages, throughout history. We played every nationality, we played children, we played animals, we played extraterrestrials and machines. We did mime, we did political satire, we sang songs. One time we did a twenty-minute fake Mozart opera, brilliantly composed by our resident composer/pianist, Bill Mathieu. Once we did a three-minute farce that took place in a Chinese restaurant. One of the actors had to leave for a few days; Tony Holland took over his part without any rehearsal, and that night the scene lasted eighteen minutes. We'd never heard such laughs. For the next few days we tried to recapture what had happened, but we were never able to.

The company became so successful that we bought the building next door to try longer, more experimental works. The first production in the new theater was a musical, a Chicago-based version of *The Threepenny Opera*, again brilliantly composed by Bill Mathieu, and it was done without a book. It had a written scenario a few pages long that the company improvised upon for several weeks, and it became a solid hit. I played MacHeath (Mack the Knife), and stayed with the show for the first couple of months. Then they hired an actor to take my place, since the first company, which now included me, would soon be leaving for New York and Broadway.

During one of my last performances (with Sills spending the days rehearsing my replacement), I came to the theater, went on, and found that I was in the wrong play. I struggled through the first act and at intermission held an impromptu meeting with the cast. "What the hell is going on?" I asked. "What play are we doing?" They told me that during the rehearsal with my replacement that afternoon, Sills got tired of the way the show was going and decided to change the story. To rewrite it. Nobody had bothered to tell me. I pleaded with the cast to do the second act as we'd rehearsed it, since I hadn't been informed of the changes and hadn't been at the rehearsal. After reviewing my desperate situation, and since Sills wasn't around that evening, the cast grudgingly agreed to do it the old way until I left Chicago, which would be a few days later. But for an hour, in front of hundreds of people, I had been in one play, the rest of the cast in another. It was the first of several classic actors' nightmares that I've lived through. There were more to follow.

CHAPTER SIX

We did not take New York by storm. We lasted on Broadway for only about three months, but during that time we developed a devoted group of fans, one of whom was Charlie Ruben, a restaurateur, who liked us so much that he decided to open a club for us in Greenwich Village. He found a place a block away from New York University, we opened, and we were an instantaneous success. We got rave reviews everywhere—newspapers, magazines, TV, and radio—and since we were a block away from New York University we had a built-in college audience right in the neighborhood. The NYU crowd was our kind of people.

A few months into our run we received another TV invitation, this time from David Susskind, who at the time had a hugely successful talk show. He wanted to devote an entire hour and a half to us, using our own format, and staying completely out of the way. We did his TV show and the next night, at the theater, we had a packed house, reservations for months to come, and a whole new uptown audience, less intellectual but with more money and better clothes. They laughed at all the right spots—all the literary references, our raised eyebrows, the pregnant pauses, the catch phrases that were the flavor of the month in local magazines or newspapers, whether they had any specific relevance to the scene or not. Being a complete snob, I left the stage one night after what seemed like a particularly self-congratulatory audience, and said in a huff, "I hate this damned bunch of pseudo-intellectuals. They don't know what the hell we're talking about, they're only laughing because they want us to know how smart they are. You mention the name Thomas Mann and you get a laugh." My next scene was with Severn Darden, one of our resident geniuses. It was a scene in which he was a sales clerk in a men's store and I was a customer trying on some clothes. Halfway through the scene I mimed putting on a new jacket, turned to Severn for his approval, and said, "How do I look?" "Wonderful!" Severn replied, and then, with a smirk, "You look just like Thomas Mann!" The audience went wild, but I felt I had been trumped by Severn, and I seethed through the rest of the evening. It was a strange new kind of experience.

One night, several months later, about five minutes before the first show, Charlie Rubin came barreling backstage. He was sweating and panting, his eyes were bulging out of his head, and there was a huge grin on his face. "Guess who's out there!" he bellowed. "Who?" we asked grudgingly, not caring all that much. "Groucho Marx!"

Now normally we didn't care a whole lot about the celebrities in the audience; most of us were still wearing our
iconoclast suits, or trying to. But Groucho was different.
He was the original iconoclast. Breaking rules was his stock
and trade. Not only that, but he'd been improvising before
anyone in this country had ever heard of the word, so we
were both honored and terribly excited to hear that he was
in the audience, and we bolted onstage with a tremendous
burst of energy. We wanted to perform for Groucho, one
of our few mentors.

Throughout the first act, the show went wildly well. The
audience was having a terrific time, I'm sure in great part
from seeing Groucho enjoying himself. About halfway into
the second act there was a scene that had been part of our
repertoire for months. The country was in the middle of
the cold war, Kennedy and Khrushchev were going at each
other hot and heavy, and our scene consisted of the two
of them fielding questions from the audience as if they
were conducting a press conference. Andrew Duncan, the
company's political expert, played Kennedy; he was knowl-
edgeable, intelligent, and witty. Zohra Lampert played a
wonderfully complex Jackie. And I played Khrushchev,
wearing, for some reason unknown to anyone including me,
one of those peaked cab driver's hats. I suppose I felt it
looked proletariat. As Khrushchev, I was able to avoid making any kind of intelligent political statement by speaking
only in Russian gibberish. In that way I could emote my
brains out without knowing a thing about politics, a topic

that interested me not at all. Severn was my translator, and it became his job to interpret my rambling histrionic nonsense and somehow make it relate to the audience's questions. That's the way it was supposed to go.

We trooped out onstage, and after Andrew made his usual introductory remarks we opened the "press conference" to the audience for questions. Immediately Groucho's hand went up. Having not much choice, Andrew pointed to him. Groucho said, "This question is for Mr. Khrushchev." I nodded. "Where did you get that hat?" he asked. I answered in my fake Russian; Severn said something in English, I think it was "Bloomingdale's." The audience laughed.

Andrew asked the audience for another question. Groucho's hand went up again. What were we to do? Andrew pointed to him. "How much was the hat?" he said. Gibberish from me. Severn said something, I forget what, but we could begin to feel where this was going and we were helpless to do anything about it. We were trapped up there. Groucho's hand went up again. "What's the material?" he asked. "Is that a wool gabardine?" Gibberish from me. Severn said something, but the handwriting was on the wall. We were beginning to come apart at the seams, and the audience loved it. Groucho kept asking question after question about the damn hat I was wearing: "Would it come in a seven and a quarter?" "Would you consider selling the one you're wearing?" By around the sixth question the audience was hysterical and so were we. We were unable to keep ourselves intact. We were all turning into Jell-O. We soon found ourselves laughing harder than the audience and finally just ran offstage in surrender. Luckily we managed to regroup in the next scene and finished the evening with a semblance of professionalism, very happy that Groucho didn't give us any more help.

He came back after the show and all of us sat with him for a couple of hours in the empty club, mostly listening to his stories in joyous rapt attention. In spite of the botched Khrushchev-Kennedy debate we seemed to have pleased Groucho, and completely out of keeping for us we actually delighted in the fact that he'd turned the show into a shambles. It was an evening none of us will ever forget, and I'm proud to say that after that night Groucho became a friend. He'd often come to see me when I was in a show in L.A., and invite me to his house for dinner, or out to a nearby restaurant. His presence was an endless source of delight to anyone who approached him. He joked with waiters, busboys, maître d's, everyone in the restaurant who came over to say hello. And more than almost anyone I've met in this business, he was inquisitive about everyone and everything. He never stopped asking questions. Once I tried to tell him of the joy he'd given me over the years and how greatly I admired him. He waved me off. "I was nothing without my brothers," he said. "Without them I wouldn't have amounted to anything."

The club in Greenwich Village stayed successful for a long time. The group, most of whom had been native Chicagoans, slowly adjusted to living in New York, and, predictably, offers for work on Broadway and in film and TV started coming in. We had considered ourselves iconoclasts and rebels, and we were a pretty tight, if dysfunctional, family. But as offers came in, things began to change. The new possibilities that were offered to some of us represented too many unspoken hopes and dreams, dreams of financial security, of greater personal recognition, of less pressured work, and the group started changing. People started leaving, new blood came in, and Second City started its long climb into becoming an institution and a success machine.

Forty years later there was a celebration and reunion in Chicago, and those of us, the early members who were still alive, climbed haltingly onstage to receive standing ovations from the crowd. We were treated like pioneers. Pathfinders. We looked at each other with our mouths open in disbelief. We had started out in Second City, all of us, because there was nowhere else to go. We were mavericks, misfits, almost unemployable. Most of the original members of the group had come out of the University of Chicago, where the dean had said publicly, "Get a general education. Don't specialize. You're all smart people; you'll end up on your feet." They took him at his word and as a result the University of Chicago produced a generation of brilliant people who wandered and floundered without finding specific work to do, all of them prospective Second City cast members. I fit right in. If anyone had told us that we were founding a dynasty, that three-quarters of the comic talent in the country for the next five decades would come from our ranks, we would have laughed in their faces. Now people join the cast in order to "make it." We did it to survive.

CHAPTER SEVEN

After being with Second City in New York for a year, I was offered a part in a Broadway play. It was called *Enter Laughing*, from a book written by Carl Reiner. It was my first Broadway play, I had the lead, and I was never off-stage. We opened in the middle of a newspaper strike, but in spite of the blackout and a complete lack of newsprint publicity, we got enough raves via television and word of mouth to turn the show into a smash hit.

The night before the reviews came out, my name was in small letters at the bottom of the ads. The next day I was over the title. As glamorous as that sounds, and as much of a dream as I thought it would be, it backfired. For the first time in my career there was no avoiding the fact that *I* was present onstage. And because the reviews singled me out, much of the audience was coming to see my work. Like it or not, I was now a celebrity, and in a couple of ways this put me under new pressures, onstage as well as off.

For the most part I had become an actor so as to hide, to find my identity through pretending to be other people. Now there was no getting around the fact that it was *me* up there in front of an audience. When I made my first entrance the audience applauded, but they were applauding the actor playing the role, stopping the show with this generous acknowledgment, a tradition in the theater but confusing and uncomfortable for me, and from that moment on I could not help feeling caught between myself and the character; I couldn't find any balance, or my way back.

In addition, I was an improvisatory actor, and not only because of the two years I'd just completed at Second City; improvisation seemed to be central to my nature. Anything else felt boring and rigid. Where was the creativity in doing a part exactly the same way every night? I know it makes sense for the playwright to have a performance set in stone; it gives the writer a feeling of security. It also makes sense and is good business for the producer—this coming Tuesday people will see the same performance they saw a year ago last September. I could see the logic in it, but I didn't want to do it.

In *Enter Laughing*, as the months went by, and as my anxieties about *being present* mounted, I also felt inhibited by the rigidity of the form. I found myself getting stale in certain parts of the play. I'd try to change the blocking just a bit, to get my juices flowing, and found that other actors onstage would actually look for me at the spot I had been the night before, where I was "supposed to be"! Then afterward there would be the inevitable notes from the stage manager, admonishing me for not sticking to the blocking.

This is a terrible confession to make; I'm aware of it. Actors are supposed to know that the play happens over and over again until the audience stops showing up. That's a given. But I can't help but ask, "Why?" Some actors are fed by the reactions of the audience, by the tiny nuances that they can add to a show over the years, by the hope of catching fire once in a while and disappearing completely into the role, by the passion generated by another actor's catching fire, by the hope that someone important will be in the house that night. Others are made secure by having someplace tangible and safe to go to instead of facing the anxieties of a random and fragmented day. None of this worked for me. Well, some of it did, for a while, in Second City, where we knew that in three months' time we'd be doing a whole new show. And yet as happy as I was at Second City, working at the top of my abilities, I was driven to explore outside that arena in the supposed magic of "Broadway." I wanted a bigger success. The irony is that I found it, and all it did was make me unhappy.

Offstage, this new identity as a known actor took some adjusting. And I didn't have much time. It began immediately after the opening-night performance of *Enter Laughing*.

After the show, since there were no newspaper reviews to wait for at Sardi's, a group of us—friends, family, and a few cast members—went across the street to a bar and had a couple of drinks while waiting for the television reviews.

The bartender flipped channels for us, and a split second after the reviews were broadcast, nearly all of them embarrassingly glowing, about eight people in the bar came rushing over with programs of the play for me to sign. Since they had programs, they had obviously been part of the audience, but they were waiting to see if I was someone whose signature was going to have any value!

It was my first view of the strange world of fandom, and with it came a moment of crystal-clear understanding. I realized that this sudden attention bestowed on me had little to do with affection for me or my work. Rather it had everything to do with people being connected to "someone of note," and for the moment I was that person. It seemed to give them a sense of stature to be associated with a "celebrity," someone who they perceived as having "done something." And they weren't even acting on their own perception. It was my acceptance by the media, a couple of three-minute reviews, that gave me stature, and their tenuous connection to me, by way of an autograph, now gave them some stature as well. It was a lesson I immediately understood, and it has stayed with me for all these years.

Although this idea of a "fan base" is part of the movie business, I really don't get it. I don't get the idea that actors think they can only do certain kinds of roles because they can't disappoint their fans. I don't get it when people say to me, about studio heads or producers, "They *love* you!" I recently asked one of my representatives not to tell me how much a casting director loved me. It's fine to tell me they like my work, but that has little to do with love. There's a dangerous illusion, I think, in the perception that the fans love us. Love is a precious thing, and I want to save discussions about it for people I've at least met.

Over the years I've done some writing, mostly children's books, but a couple of pieces for adults as well, and on occasion I've received letters from people who have read my work. Invariably they are notes of thanks and gratitude for my having given them something. But the world of show business is different. For some reason people who make movies are seen as public property. The impression is that in exchange for our celebrity we owe the fans something. They want our signature on 3-by-5 cards, and often not just one card but several. They want signatures on photographs, which they will sometimes provide, but often not, as if part of our job is to supply endless images of ourselves. There are requests for messages to loved ones on birthdays or anniversaries. There are endless questionnaires, both personal and professional. Over the past forty years I have had perhaps fifteen or twenty letters of thanks from people who feel that my work has in some way been a gift, and for these I am truly grateful. But those letters, although treasured, are few and far between. It's as if what we do on screen or in the theater isn't work at all but rather some fairytale imagined existence, and part of our job is to impart our secret and magical life to anyone who can get close enough to ask. No one seems to pay attention to how difficult a life it can be, and how many broken, fragmented lives are connected to it, a sad fact that seems endemic to the world of show business. Add to this the fact that for a great many of us our work is a serious addiction, with all of the liabilities that accompany any dangerous addiction. Yet in our culture it can seem, to those looking on, that we are "only playing." Only fooling around.

I've often felt that there could be a fun coffee-table book of exchanges between fans and celebrities. A few, which I've heard about from colleagues over the years, have been priceless. One of my favorite stories was one Eli Wallach told me years ago. He was in a Broadway show at the time, and one Sunday morning he was leaving Zabar's loaded down with a couple of shopping bags filled with the usual New York Sunday-morning fare, when a lady grabbed him by the arm, stopping him cold and whipping him around. Holding him was a middle-aged woman staring at him intently, a big smile on her face. "I know you!" she said, wagging a finger. "Don't tell me, don't tell me," she said, holding him captive in a vice-like grip. Eli loves attention, and is very good with people, so he waited patiently while she consulted the rolodex in her head of people he could have been. "Telly Savalas!" she finally blurted out. Eli said no. "Martin Balsam!" She yelled out the name as if she'd just won at bingo. Eli said no. "Peter Falk!" No, said Eli. "Efrem Zimbalist Jr.!" No. "Ben Gazzara!" No. Finally the woman gave up. "Who are you?" she demanded. "I'm Eli Wallach." The woman clutched her heart; a beatific smile came over her face. "My favorite!" she said and walked away.

Tony Perkins told me about a time when he was sitting in the back of a cab—it was during a lull in his career—and saw the driver scrutinizing him in the rear-view mirror. After a while the cabbie, unable to contain himself, said, "Excuse me, but didn't you used to be Tony Perkins?"

My favorite anecdote involving me took place years ago when I was on location, making a film. We'd stopped to shoot in Nashville for a couple of days, and one night a group of us went to dinner at what we heard was a good Italian restaurant. In the middle of the meal the maître d' came over to me and said in a thick Italian accent, "I saw you in the movies last night." "I don't think you did," I answered. I hadn't done anything in a while, and nothing of mine was in theaters anywhere. "Yes I did," he said again. "Last night I saw you in the movies." "I don't think so," I said, wanting to get back to my dinner. "Nothing of mine is playing in town," I told him and turned away. Not taking the hint, the maître d' said, "I never forget a face. I saw you last night in *Diary of a Mad Housewife.*" "I wasn't in *Diary of a Mad Housewife,*" I said, starting to get annoyed. "Yes you were," insisted the maître d'. "Look," I said, now a bit steamed. "I know what I was in and what I wasn't in, and I wasn't in *Diary of a Mad Housewife.*" "Yes you were," the maître d' repeated. "No I wasn't!" I said, churning. "Yes," he said. "I'll tell you where." "Okay," I said, giving in, and he went on: "I saw you sitting on the steps of the theater before the movie started. You were talking to a boy who was about twelve years old." And he had me. I had gone to see the movie the night before with my son Adam, and we had sat on the steps of the theater to talk for a few minutes before the film began. "You got me," I said. "So what are you doing in town?" the maître d' asked me, now that we were pals. "I'm a traveling salesman," I said, "just passing through."

It's a strange life. But I'm in a good place in it. I'm a character actor. I don't get mobbed; I can go anywhere and not feel as if my privacy is going to be intruded on. When I am approached in public these days it's most often by people who have liked something I've done, and the exchanges tend to be fun and respectful. And once in a while I'm given a better seat on an airplane.

CHAPTER EIGHT

During the year at Second City in New York, and then throughout my run in *Enter Laughing*, even though everything was going exceedingly well professionally I had no life outside the theater. For all the good I did anyone I could have been hung up in a closet somewhere. In one memorable week three different people suggested that I should go into analysis. It was a wake-up call and I listened.

I had no idea what to expect from analysis. I didn't know anyone who'd ever experienced it. During the first month I told the doctor a dream I had.

"It was terrible," I said. "My brother Bob fell into a bear pit and the bars around the cage were too high for me to get in and save him. My poor brother. He was killed by the bears."

"Who threw him in the bear pit?" the doctor said.

"Not me," I answered.

"No?" the doctor asked. "Who had the dream?"

It was as if I'd been hit in the head with a two-by-four. I had the dream. There was someone inside. There was something going on within me that caused things to happen, things that I generated, in my personal life as well as my professional life. I had an identity. For my first thirty years I had marveled at my own acts as if they were created by some external power, as if I were a bystander to my own behavior. In spite of all the analysis I had done on characters I'd been playing, I had never given a thought to my own internal life, or whether I even had one. Like many people I saw myself as a force of nature that I had almost no control over, as an innocent bystander to my own life. With this one comment from my doctor, and my ability to recognize its implications, self-discovery became a second obsession.

There was a lot of work to do, plenty of bad behavior to get over. Having called myself an "artist" since I was five, I had a lot of examples to re-examine. "Well," I'd say to myself, "Beethoven was a boor, but look what he gave to the world." Or, "Mozart was irresponsible and childish, so what? Who would have him any other way? He was charming! He was mysterious! He made generations of people happy!" Excuse after excuse to be antisocial or selfish. The history books might forgive me, I thought at the time, while I was fantasizing my obituary, but I could no longer forgive myself for my inadequacies. They began to eat at me. And it started to become clear to me that I was alive in the present moment, and only then. Not in reviews, not in photographs, not in my interviews or my imagined biographies, but right there in the moments that I drew breath and my heart was beating. The rest was ephemeral nonsense.

I stayed in *Enter Laughing* for a year. After my contract ended I went back to Second City for two months and then back on Broadway again to be in Murray Schisgal's wonderful three-character play *Luv*, along with Eli Wallach and Anne Jackson. It too was a hit, and I remained in it for a year.

At the end of my commitment to *Luv*, I had my first screen test. It was for the part of a submarine officer in *The Russians Are Coming*. I told Norman Jewison, the director, that I'd do a screen test, but only if I could improvise it. He said okay, and I did the screen test, improvising several scenes, working off Norman who stayed behind the camera. I got the part and we did the film.

One of the things that attracted me to the project was its strong social statement. We were smack in the middle of the cold war at the time, and the film had the audacious message that Russians were human beings, pretty much like us. It sounds inane now, but at that moment in our history the Soviet Union was so demonized that making a movie that challenged that view was actually a pretty courageous thing to do. I think most of us in the cast were in accord with that mission, and it helped us bond as a group.

We very much expected a backlash of some kind, but to our amazement and delight, when the film came out, it was as if the whole country breathed a sigh of relief. The relief was reflected in the reviews, and in the way people approached us—there was no backlash at all. It turned out that most of the country seemed to feel the same way we did, and hadn't had the courage to come out and say it.

Norman spoiled me for most of the directors who I worked with after him. He loved actors and had no difficulty showing his appreciation for good work. He was also passionate about the script and its statement, and unlike most directors, who lock themselves and a few cronies in the screening room to look at dailies, Norman showed his dailies in the local movie theater and he invited the entire town. People would show up with their dogs, their babies, their grandparents, the halt and the lame, and every couple of weeks Norman would have to stand up in his seat and yell to the assembled town, "People, I'm going to have to ask you to leave your babies and dogs at home, because we can't hear the sound track!" Everyone would comply for a few days and then he'd have to make the speech again.

During shooting, at the end of a scene Norman would sometimes let the camera keep rolling to see what would happen. In my zeal I just kept going until I heard him say "cut," and as a result there is some improvisation in the film that had little to do with my desire to add to the material; I just didn't want to make any mistakes. I didn't hear anyone say "cut," so I kept talking. I was desperate to do everything right.

From the beginning, film felt like the medium I had been waiting for. There was none of the terrible pressure of working in front of an audience and none of the endless grind of a long run. We'd work on a scene until it felt right and then go on to the next one. Making movies was the answer to my prayers.

It lasted half a decade. For about five years I had a pretty successful run of films; then, for no reason I could determine, my career took a dip. This is not an infrequent occurrence in an actor's life. No matter how smoothly things are going, the tide comes in, the tide goes out. It's not pleasant, and it tends to feels personal. And if you're not careful, it's easy to start blaming people for it.

When it happened to me I continued to get work, but offers came less often, with scripts that I didn't love, and with directors who did not enthrall me. This is a part of my past that I am not terribly proud of—my difficulty dealing with people in positions of authority, for whom I had no respect. If I was faced with a director who I thought was incompetent or cruel, I would become insufferable and I would not communicate. If he gave me an idea I didn't like, I would dismiss it abruptly, often rudely.

This grandiose attitude of mine went on for a couple of years, during which time I was offered the lead in a film called *Popi*, a biting social satire about the plight of Puerto

Ricans in New York. It made a wonderful statement and, finally, I was getting a chance to play a rich and complex character, exactly the kind of material I wanted to do.

Halfway through the film we had to do a scene that involved the decapitation of a pigeon. It was an ugly and violent moment, but it wasn't gratuitous; it had meaning in context of the film. In the scene the decapitated pigeon was going to be used to taunt my two children, and was meant to point up some of the barbarism that the kids were exposed to in their lives. Minutes before the scene was to be shot I asked the assistant director how they were going to film cutting the head off the pigeon. He said, "They're just going to do it. They're going to cut the head off the pigeon."

I hit the roof. I ran over to the producers. "What the hell are you doing?" I yelled. "You're going to show how awful violence is by committing violence? What are you, crazy?" I threatened them, I screamed obscenities, and I ultimately bullied them into finding another method for depicting the scene, which they grudgingly did, unhappy about slowing down the schedule but more afraid of my anger and threats. It was a time in my life when I was unsure of how to handle my position in a film. I felt, sometimes too vehemently, that since I was in a position of at least some leadership I needed to champion the rights of the other people involved, and in this case even animals who were not in a position to speak for themselves. In *Popi* I had already taken it upon myself to make demands on behalf of some of the extras working on the film, and also some of the people from whom we'd rented apartments in Spanish Harlem to use as sets, all of whom felt they'd been treated unfairly by the producers. The pigeon was the last straw.

After I cooled down and had a chance to think about what had taken place, I was struck by the several levels of irony contained in the event. Here was a scene devoted to pointing a finger at man's barbarity, and in depicting it, by killing the pigeon, we were going to use the same cruel methods we were decrying in the script. But to add to the knot of ironies, to stop the producer's callousness and cruelty I had flown into a bullying rage, adding my own brand of inhumanity to the mess we were concocting.

It felt like layer upon layer of confusion, and the incident resounded in me for a long time.

I sought clarity by visiting a trusted teacher. He knew me well—my easy ability to find outrage in the injustices of the world as well as in the shortcomings of others. He knew my sense of self-righteousness and my temper. At the moment of this visit I was also complaining about the lousy notes I was getting from a particular director, who I didn't respect at all, and how I wasn't following them. He heard my grievance and said, "It might be interesting to try to follow his directions. See what happens."

His response shocked me. Why should I listen to the ideas of a director who was completely incompetent? His credits were nowhere as impressive as mine. I had major awards, what had he done? I didn't understand why I was being instructed to follow the directions of someone who was clearly not up to my exacting standards. But at that time I found it wise to abide by this trusted teacher's instructions, whether I understood them or not. So for the rest of that film, in fact for several films after, I vowed to put my own ego aside and try every idea that a director would throw at me.

And interesting things started to happen. Often the idea was indeed terrible, and when I attempted to perform it to the best of my ability, it just didn't work. But sometimes it did work. And my performance was better for it, and the film was improved. And the distinction between the good ideas and the bad ones was always clear.

Then other things started to happen that were even more important. First, as a result of my resolve to cooperate, my relationships with directors improved. I realized that a few of them had been afraid of me; this was no longer the case. We were now allies, and though I still might have reservations about their talent, they were colleagues with whom I could have a civilized and productive dialogue, and together we could steer the film in a direction that could excite us both. This was a lesson that stood me in good stead, both in my profession and in my personal life.

The lesson of the pigeon stayed with me as well.

I was about five years into therapy, and while my work with my doctor was tearing down walls in my emotional life, it was also opening a window into the wall that had separated my professional and personal lives. I had never thought of myself as a violent person, but now I was confronted with the daunting task of recognizing that the in-humanity I was so eager to denounce in the *Popi* script was alive and well in me.

The realization ate at me, and I finally saw that I could no longer allow myself to feel this great self-congratulatory surge that I see in so many artists who have participated in a work that has some social value. I have seen the irony played out too often—the thinking is that since they have done something deeply significant and even courageous in "bringing this important message to the screen," they are allowed some special license in their own behaviors, and I wonder how many acts of selfishness and mindlessness have been perpetrated on co-workers, family members, and em-ployees to get the humanitarian message across, and how much money has been made in the process.

We live with the illusion that the ends are worth the means. That in art, the message in the final product will jus-tify the lack of humanity that took place during the making of the work. In this period, for reasons I still don't under-stand, I started to see the discrepancies not only in others but in myself as well, and I could no longer allow myself to get away with that kind of behavior. When I caught myself acting that way, and it was more often than I wanted to ad-mit, it stayed with me and I suffered for it. My memory could no longer rub out the moments of cruelty and cal-lousness I'd perpetrated on others because of some pursuit that seemed noble in my own mind, the ends being more important than the means, and what I discovered, finally, is that there are no ends. What seem like ends are simply arbitrary signposts we put up for ourselves in order to make us comfortable, to give ourselves the illusion that we are finished with something. The blessing of the event with the pigeon was that it had rubbed my nose in my own complicity in this behavior, and I could no longer allow myself to get away with it.

CHAPTER NINE

After about five years of intense work with my therapist, I began to feel that analysis had its limitations. It helped me get rid of some fears, and it opened my eyes to an interior life, but I was starting to come up against things for which Freud didn't seem to have answers, or even any interest. I started having deep and significant breakthroughs that took me into other realities. I had several dramatic experiences that suggested strongly the possibility of other lives, which were disconcerting to say the least, but were as tangible and transforming as anything I'd ever experienced, and my doctor, who was a good and responsible man, couldn't help me with what I was discovering. In addition, when confronting him with issues that didn't seem to be solvable, he'd come back with "Well, that's the human condition," or some statement that was the equivalent of "Well, I never promised you a rose garden." This idea infuriated me. The suggestion that the best we could hope for in our personal lives was settling for endless disappointment and mediocrity sounded like a cop-out. He might not have promised me a rose garden, but there were people out there who had rose gardens, and I wanted one. Occasionally I'd meet people and see a look in their eyes that told me they'd achieved some sort of peace and joy, some ability to relax into themselves, and it made me feel hungry and envious. If it was possible for someone else, it was possible for me.

Shortly after finishing the filming of *Catch-22* I began reading a lot of Eastern philosophy, Buddhist and Vedantic, mostly, and I also started meditating. The transformations that took place from these new levels of awareness were dramatic, sometimes frightening, often disorienting, and changed me so much that within a couple of years I began not to recognize myself. There was a great shift in my philosophy and belief systems, but the intellectual aspects of the changes were only interesting sidelights compared to the fundamental changes that took place within me, tangible, physical changes in my body along with a deeper awareness of the world within and around me.

For example, there was an occasion about three years into my early work with my first meditation teacher when I woke up in the middle of the night feeling as if my heart had exploded. I had never had any concern about my heart, never had any pathology, but I was sure I was having a heart attack. For some reason, instead of calling a doctor I called my teacher and asked him if I should rush to a hospital. Instead of pointing me to the nearest emergency room, he congratulated me. "Your heart has opened," he said. "It's a great blessing. Relax and enjoy it."

Now I don't recommend that everyone who feels their heart "explode" follow this advice—but in my case, at that moment, and given my new awareness of mind and body, I relaxed into the sensation and within half an hour the explosive feelings in my chest subsided, yet for many months afterward I felt out of balance.

There was a new heat in the middle of my chest, and my center of gravity went through a shift; even my posture changed. I was living in a new place inside my body and it took a long time to adjust to what was feeling like a new me.

I had read a lot of material in mystical literature on the seven vortexes in our bodies, and learned that a good part of our work is to awaken these vortexes, but reading about them was like reading science fiction, interesting conceptually, but who the hell knew if it was true? There was no way to verify any of it. Before the heart episode I had no place to put any of that exciting but far-out information. Now I did, but it required that I rethink who I was because the new sensations in my chest were insisting that I react in new ways to almost all the situations in my life. It also meant that to a certain extent I needed to re-examine my acting technique.

There was an actor named Michael Chekhov, popular in the 1930s, who had also been an acting teacher of some reputation. He had stumbled onto the theory of these psychic centers, these vortexes, intuitively I suppose, and he used this idea as part of his teaching method. His idea was that each of us is locked up in certain parts of our bodies and open in others, and that most of us are focused in one particular spot. People with energy focused in their lower back would feel and act a certain way, their emotional lives reflecting this specific weight and concentration. People who are focused in their throats would behave in another way. People in their hearts, yet another. Playing with this idea, thinking of myself as being weighted or having more life in one specific area of my body, immediately gave me a completely different sense of who I was, emotionally as well as in essence. In imitating people, which I'd done since I was a kid, I realized that I'd been using Chekhov's method intuitively for most of my life. Now with my heart having exploded open and being forced to live more fully in that area, I realized for the first time that this place within me had been closed all my life. Now I was thrust into feeling myself in a new way.

At first it was disconcerting and frightening. The heart, from a metaphysical standpoint, is just what you would expect it to be, a place of love and connection and vulnerability. Somewhere along the line I had shut it down, for my own reasons, and I didn't particularly enjoy this new vulnerability, not to mention its effect on my instincts about a character I might be playing.

The new sensations threw me for a loop. It took many months to readjust to the new me, and once I did, a new opening took place somewhere else in my system that would require seeing myself in yet another light, and once again this would force me into adjusting to a new physical center of gravity. This has continued to happen right up to the present. Not as dramatically as that first experience with the heart, but dramatically enough so that my sense of myself as an entity, an energy field, has become fluid rather than fixed. Our energetic perception of ourselves is as profound a statement of who we are as anything else about us, and each time these energy fields go through a transmutation, a shift, we have to re-examine ourselves. We feel differently, within ourselves and in our relationship to the outside world. And when we feel differently we behave differently, and when we behave differently, as actors, we have to change our techniques, our approaches to our work, the places we work from.

When I did *Catch-22*, I worked with Tony Perkins, who was a delightful, kind, and literate man. For some reason the moment he appeared before a camera things became painful for him. Just before the word "action," Tony would unfailingly say, "Oh God, where did I go wrong." It was the place he worked from. He needed, for whatever reason, a sense of shame, or discomfort, or self-judgment that took him to the place he felt he needed to act from.

When I worked with Jack Lemmon on *Glengarry Glen Ross*, Jack would say before every single take, "It's magic time!" That was the place he worked from. It was what propelled him into his acting place.

Another way to approach the work was told to me by my son Matthew, when he was studying with Uta Hagen, who, along with being a brilliant actress, was one of the most revered acting teachers in New York. Matt told me that his first months with her were horrible; it was like listening to my criticism of him all over again.

He went on to say, "Time and again I'd play a scene with a partner, and afterward Uta would ask, 'What can you tell me about what happened?' And I would tell her what I thought went right with the scene, what I had so carefully planned to achieve, what I felt I had properly executed. And she would listen and nod, and tell me it was very good, and showed a thorough understanding of character, circumstance, and objective, but that it all seemed planned and she could tell that I knew what was coming next. And I wanted to scream at her, as I so often wanted to scream at you, 'Of course I know what's coming next. I read the play! I've worked on the scene for two, three, four weeks!'"

Finally, in frustration and rage, Matt decided to show her. He was going to bring in a scene that he had done twice already, and he wasn't going to do a damn thing. He was going to sit there and listen to his partner, and say the words, and nothing else. He was not going to inflect, he was not going to express an emotion or have a goal, nothing other than to show Uta that if you don't plan what to do next, nothing will happen.

The scene began. Matt sat on the couch, sullen, listening to the other actor. But then, he told me, something odd happened.

"My heart started to race. I began to sweat and shake. I felt confused, and frightened, as if I was in the middle of a big lake at night, with no idea of the direction to the shore. I started to respond to the other character because I had to, because there was nothing else to do. Somehow, the scene made it to its end. Uta asked, 'What can you tell me?'"

"It was terrible," I replied.

"Why?"

"Because I didn't know what was going on, I didn't have any plan, I didn't know what was going to happen from one moment to the next."

"And," she said, "it was the best work you have ever done in class. And you have done some good work."

"But I was incredibly uncomfortable."

Uta paused and looked at me sweetly (to which she was not given—she was not sentimental), before saying, "Oh my dear boy. Who ever told you that you were supposed to be comfortable?"

My suspicion is that Ms. Hagen was referring to the discomfort of the character, and not that Matt was supposed to be in a state of discomfort onstage for the rest of his life. At any rate, that was Matt's breakthrough as an actor, and it involved his dramatically changing the place he worked from. He understood the power of story; that truths want to be told, have a will to be told, and that if we can simply exist in the scene the story and its truth will pass through us, willing itself into existence. It is our job only to *be* in the scene, to have the experience. That is what audiences come to see. Of course it's not a bad idea to be playing the character while all this is going on.

One of the things that happens after an actor has had an experience such as Matthew's is that technique can come into play. It then becomes possible to remember the initial experience, and how you got there, and to create a close semblance of the event, so that in a long run you don't become an emotional wreck by actually living the experience night after night. Because like it or not, the character and his feelings become your feelings. I guess a lot of actors from other traditions might feel otherwise, but I think the emotions and the essence of the character dig into us, whether we like it or not.

I remember Carol Burnett telling me that she'd been invited by Dr. Thelma Moss, a professor at UCLA, to try an experiment in the Kirlian aura lab. Carol was asked to place her hand on a photographic plate. A picture was taken by some technique that showed an aura around the hand, and apparently each person's aura is unique. Carol was then asked to do a series of photographs where she was to *think*, just *think* of herself as each of about a half-dozen of the characters she was known for. On every occasion the resulting photograph was significantly different from either Carol's personal imprint or those of her other characters. When Dr. Moss looked at the photographs she described, in detail, the emotional life of the characters that Carol was thinking of at the time. Carol said that in each case her description of the character was spot-on. This was a pretty graphic demonstration of how thought, and the way we *think* of ourselves, becomes a dynamic that influences our many systems, and in many different ways, onstage and in life as well.

For many years my acting came from a place of surmounting some enormous obstacle, confronting some stern and faceless judge who would condemn me to a pit of hell if I didn't achieve the "zone," if even for a moment. Not a particularly happy place to work from. But as my interior work started taking me over, as the sensibility within me started to shift and change, I could no longer hang on to that stance.

Through my early years in front of a camera there had been no life whatsoever outside of my tightly focused eyeline. There was no crew, no director; there were only the specific actors I was working with. I was intensely focused on my subjects, and this came out of a ferocious attachment to my acting technique, which protected me from my own fears and a terrible sense of being judged, of being disliked, of needing approval. Now, as things started to crack open inside of me, as these centers began to open, I lost that tight focus. I would play a scene, working to the best of my ability, and no matter how hard I tried I could not shut out what was taking place in my peripheral vision—the knowledge that a crew was present, with a director behind the camera, and a lot of lights and trucks just off the set. When that began to happen I felt as if I were losing my ability to act altogether. I would sheepishly check with the director to see if he'd noticed anything wrong with my performance. No one ever said a word. Then I would realize that for better or worse I had to incorporate my expanded sense of awareness into my technique. I wasn't particularly happy about it, but there didn't seem to be anything else to do, so I lived with it, feeling that my abilities as an actor had diminished to some extent. I had to accept it. There was no other choice.

Then, one day, I was reading a book by a Native American shaman and I came across a chapter on vision. The shaman maintained that as one's consciousness expanded one's vision got broader. Literally. One's field of vision actually grew wider. He went on to say that tight vision belongs to a world of confrontation, to the hunter, and broad vision to a world of wider and more subtle perceptions. He also maintained that as one became used to this breadth of vision, the details of the tight vision could be sustained while everything else in the periphery continues to be seen and acknowledged. I had never encountered this idea before, and it gave me a sense, for the first time, that what was happening to me was constructive and developmental, and not just a sign that my acting ability was going down the drain. Nevertheless, I had to relearn how to act. I had to redefine who I was when I was playing a character. My work had to become more public, more accepting of the real world around me that was going on at the same time I was playing a scene. But there is a strange and interesting phenomenon that takes place within our psyches. As was the case with Matt's experience with Uta, and my own experience with expanding vision and many other such experiences, all of which were very positive indications of growth, initially and almost invariably they feel like aberrations. Like failings! In almost every case I've felt that there was something wrong with me, and it's taken some time to adjust to the idea that: "Hey, this is good! I'm in a better place!" An odd state of affairs.

Another one of these shifts took place while I was doing *The In-Laws*. During the shooting, for the first time in my life I found myself having a good time while working. There was nothing I could do about it. There was no struggle involved, no mountain to climb. Out of nowhere, acting had become play, and for weeks I worried that I might get fired. Before *The In-Laws* I had felt that I had to work my ass off to get into some kind of state, into the zone, shot by shot, in order to do acceptable work. Now, in spite of myself, I was having fun.

For the first weeks of shooting I tried to jam myself into my old familiar work place. I tried to suffer, to constrict myself; I couldn't make it happen. I kept looking at the director, Arthur Hiller, to see if he was disapproving, to see if he knew the terrible fact that I was *having fun* and not *working*. I looked at Peter Falk, my co-star, to see if he was hating me for enjoying myself; no one said anything. In fact, people seemed to like it. I even think my having fun allowed Peter to do the same. I'm not sure that it's a place he's frequented too often in his career. He's a terrific actor, but I don't think *fun* is a word that he would apply to his work process.

Interestingly, over the years when people talk to me about *The In-Laws*, the first thing they say to me—and this has happened not once but literally hundreds of times—the first thing they say is, "God, it looks like you guys are having a good time in that film." And more perplexing yet, it seems to mean something to them. When I answer, "Yes, we had a ball making *The In-Laws*," I see people breathe a sigh of relief. It has happened over and over again, and after the fiftieth or hundredth time that someone said those words to me I began to wonder why they cared. What difference could it possibly make to anyone whether or not I had a good time making *The In-Laws*, or any other film for that matter? There are a few other movies I've made over the years that received similar responses from audiences, and amazingly it's invariably the films in which I *was* having a good time that prompted people to ask me this question. These audiences of one always knew, and they always cared, and they always breathed a sigh of relief when I said "yes."

And then I began noticing that I do the same thing with my favorite films or favorite musical groups. When I find out that the musicians of a string quartet that I've admired for years fight endlessly with each other, it fills me with inexplicable sadness. When I meet other actors and ask them about their experience in a film, wondering if it had been fun to make, if I get a positive response it fills me with joy. This strange phenomenon puzzled me. Either people enjoyed the movie or they didn't. Is everyone that much of a Samaritan that they need me to have a good time while I'm acting? I don't think so, but I couldn't find an explanation for it. It puzzled me for years until one day I tried an experiment in order to solve another problem of mine, and it took care of both of them at the same time.

I've always loved classical music, and I've always loved Carnegie Hall. Yet for years, getting myself to a concert there filled me with dread. It happened over and over again, and try as I might I couldn't make any sense of it. Over the years it began to really annoy me. I only went to Carnegie Hall to hear music I loved, no one forced me to attend, it was always of my own volition, and yet each time I got near the place I'd struggle with terrible anxiety. I berated myself endlessly about it but never came to an understanding of what the cause could possibly be.

One night, thoroughly fed up with myself, I determined to get to the bottom of it. There was a performance of Beethoven's 9th taking place at Carnegie Hall, which I'd been looking forward to for several weeks. I asked a couple of friends to come with me. It was a performance by an orchestra I'd been a fan of for many years through recordings, but had never seen. I told my friends about my problem and said I wanted to go with them as if I were blind. I thought limiting my senses and allowing myself to be cared for might relax me enough to get a handle on what was bothering me.

My friends agreed. I put on a pair of dark glasses and off we went to Carnegie Hall. I was fine until we neared the auditorium. As we got within earshot of the place, I began to pick up the excitement of the people waiting in the lobby for the auditorium to open. I began to hear snatches of conversation and also began to pick up the jarring collisions of emotional states of those waiting to get in. I could hear it and I could feel it. A lot of people were waiting with great enthusiasm. Others didn't really want to be there; they were there to appease a date, a husband or a wife. Others were there because it was a corporate gift and felt they had to attend. Others went to keep a scorecard. They'd heard different orchestras perform the 9th and they were there to evaluate nuances of this orchestra, pitting it against the others, showing off their knowledge and hoping to add another notch to their expertise. Some attending the concert were musicians; they had friends who were playing that night. Others were present because it was their outing for the evening—tomorrow it would be the opera, the next day the ballet, in a continuous fix of culture.

I felt barraged with the endlessly varied agendas of the people who were attending, and I quickly realized this is what had been driving me nuts over the years—the cacophony of egos and personal needs. I was desperate for some silence. Some sense of awe, of humble anticipation of what might be coming. The doors of the auditorium eventually opened and we were let in, and the lot of us scrambled for our seats, talking, complaining, rummaging through programs, trying to figure out where to stash our stuff, oddly girding ourselves against the onslaught of the Beethoven, most of us doing everything possible to avoid the chance of open connection, or confrontation with what was before us.

The music started. I stayed blind, trying for once to feel the entire experience rather than attempting to block out the audience, or anything else that I might have considered extraneous. I wanted to feel everything going on, not just the music onstage but everything happening in the hall. As the music continued the audience slowly began to settle down, and it soon became clear that we were hearing an extraordinary performance of the 9th. The orchestra was on fire. About five minutes into the first movement, the varied personal agendas in the audience began to melt down and then slowly disappear, all agendas, those of audience and musicians alike, until finally the only purpose or meaning in the hall was Beethoven's. And then by the end of the third movement even Beethoven's agenda was gone, and we were swept up in what *he* had been swept up by, what lived through him, and all of Carnegie Hall became one living organism, one thing with a couple thousand moving parts. We had let go, and we lived inside that majestic vision of brotherhood and unity and heroism written over two hundred years ago.

We had become the music.

When the piece finished, when the applause died down, there was a split second of recognition of what had taken place. I could sense a subterranean desire sweep through the audience to hang on to this connection that had been forced on us by the music, this unearthly unity and love that Beethoven's music *insists* on. For a split second you could feel in the audience a need to join hands and link together and look each other in the face, or grab each other and embrace, a need to apologize for a lifetime of neglect, to cry, to tell each person in the hall that we would always love them, that we always *had* loved them.

And then the moment was over. And slowly the discussions began, the intellectualizations, the looking for overcoats, the program searches, the rush to the restaurants and garages. And I took off my dark glasses and finally knew what my anxiety had been about. For me, going to Carnegie Hall had always been going to church. I knew that what I would find there, in those rare, exalted moments, would be a holy experience. I went there to abandon myself to the power not only of the music but, even more importantly, to the occasional unity that presents itself when a group of artists catch fire and become one thing. When what rules the evening is the essence of the music, not the people playing, or those listening to it. And I began to realize that the underlying message that runs through all of the group art forms, whether it be dance, music, theater, or film, is: "Look at us! We can get along! We can do this beautiful thing and we are doing it together and actually *enjoying* each other! There is hope for us after all!"

This is the message that runs underneath and through all the group art forms. I don't know what else would explain an audience's desperate need to know that they'd been part of something grand and joyous and unifying, or even to know that an actor had fun making a movie. And I find myself thinking, my God, if we can't get along playing music, dancing, singing, pretending we're other people, what possible hope is there for the people who work at the U.N.? For doctors? For research scientists? For teachers? For all those places and professions where lives are at stake? What we do as performers *has* to be joyous and it *has* to be generous. The audience needs to know.

CHAPTER TEN

Somewhere along the way I became a director. It was not part of my life plan, nor was it a profession I thought I had any particular talent for. I never thought of myself as a leader and I didn't want to be one.

But one day I got a call from a couple of friends who were in rehearsal for an off-Broadway play. They said the cast was foundering under bad leadership, and they asked if I would consider coming in and taking over the direction. I wasn't working at the time so I said I'd take a look at a rehearsal and see what I thought.

I went to the theater and watched a run-through, completely confused about what I was seeing. The play made no sense to me, and without a handle on what it was supposed to be about I felt I couldn't be of much help. They thanked me for coming in, and I went home. Two weeks later they called again. They'd hired a second director, and after a few days he turned out to be as bad as the first. Would I come in again and take another look?

I went back and watched another run-through. This time, although I still felt the play wasn't working and the acting stiff, I could at least follow the plot, even though I didn't understand it. I had nothing else on my plate at the time and I liked the idea of helping my friends in the show, so I said I'd take over. With my heart in my mouth I started rehearsals. I had no craft as a director and no idea of where to begin, so I sat there and watched. All I knew was that I could determine when something felt false or incomprehensible to me.

To my surprise, when I made suggestions, the actors would actually try them. When they'd ask me why I was telling them to do certain things, I found to my further surprise that I could come up with reasons that satisfied them. As the days went on I began to enjoy my new hat, and I found that as the newly clarified moments in the play piled up on each other it all started making sense. To my delight, I discovered that it was quite funny. The play opened, ran for a year, and I started getting some off-Broadway directorial work.

At every opportunity, I would hire the actors I'd worked with at Second City. My second play was *Little Murders*, by Jules Feiffer. Two of the cast members were from Second City, Andrew Duncan and Fred Willard. Then came *The White House Murder Case*, also by Jules Feiffer, and once more most of the cast was from Second City: Andrew Duncan, again, who as far as I was concerned was the unsung hero of Second City, Anthony Holland, J. J. Barry, Paul

Dooley, and Peter Bonerz, who was from another successful improv group called The Committee.

Whenever I work with actors with improvisational training, my rehearsal time is cut in half. It's been my experience that a lot of actors don't really read scripts. They read their parts and pay only cursory attention to the other elements of the play. As a result they don't know their function within the totality of the event, and it becomes a director's job to fit the actor into the piece as a whole. Actors with improvisational training almost always understand the shape of the event they're working within. I think it's at least in part because improvisational actors are simultaneously their own writers and directors. When you've improvised long enough you develop instincts—about the style of the piece you're working in, but also about when to take over, when to step back, where to position yourself physically onstage while leaving room for the other actors, when to come on and when to get off. Since no one is in charge, generosity becomes a survival technique. These skills transfer easily into working on written material. Most actors bury their heads in the role, forgetting that in a well-constructed piece each role has a function. Being aware of that function makes finding the character that much easier, and good improvisational actors tend to excel at knowing their function within the whole.

Improvisation became a natural tool and I used it frequently as a director, particularly when a scene wasn't making sense to the actors. When this happened I'd look for an improvisational "paraphrase" for the scene—a completely different situation for the actors, but one containing the same emotional essence. Oddly enough, the paraphrase could sometimes be completely transparent, and the actors would not see it. In working on the essence of the scene in this way, almost invariably what actors discovered in the new situation could be translated back into the text.

My favorite example of this took place while we were rehearsing *Little Murders*. There is a scene in the play where the Newquist family is being introduced to their daughter's new fiancé, Alfred. Alfred comes into the home with his bride-to-be and the family makes a great show of accepting their prospective son-in-law. Alfred stays totally uncommunicative, giving the family nothing in the way of social graces, and the tension mounts. What I wanted was for the Newquists to become more and more forced as their efforts turned to nothing. I wanted their gaiety and the party atmosphere to turn hollow and theatrical. The actors had trouble achieving this effect, and I felt the reason was that good actors instinctively don't want to look false. What I was asking them to do seemed to go against their instincts and years of training. But I've always loved to watch people performing in real life. I get a kick out of the faces people put on that often have nothing to do with what's taking place inside. As much as it happens in life, this is difficult to pull off theatrically because false simply tends to look false. But in this case it felt very much needed, so I decided to try an improv. I told the family, Elizabeth Wilson, Jon Korkes,

Vince Gardenia, and Linda Lavin, that the president of the United States had decided that as a Christmas present to the country he was going to pay a special visit to a hand-picked American family. Then I took aside Fred Willard, who was playing Alfred, and told him that when he came in with his entourage he should say and do absolutely nothing. The improv started and I watched as the family prepared for the president's visit with intense anticipation and excitement. Then Fred came in with his people and he stood there. Smiling. Giving the family nothing. The family started out the scene in a state of genuine excitement, and within a few minutes you could see them beginning to strain, working at their joy. They tried everything they could think of to warm him up, to get him to react. Anything. Fred did nothing. After about ten minutes their enthusiasm became false and hollow, their smiles painful, their laughs more like coughs. Another five minutes and they fell on the floor exhausted, laughing their heads off. They got the paraphrase completely, and through the many months that they performed the play they never lost it. What was interesting to me was the transparency of the improv. It was so close to the content of the scene in the play that it was almost impossible not to see through it, but they didn't, and the improv worked exactly as I hoped it would.

CHAPTER ELEVEN

There is an unconscious ritual that actors go through in nearly every play I've directed. We'll have been rehearsing the play for about three weeks, and during a break an actor will come up to me in a state of intense agitation and say, "I can't understand this scene; it's driving me crazy. I don't know what the character is doing here. I'm at a complete loss, and I feel completely hamstrung." My inevitable answer is "You're playing the scene right now." The actor stops in his tracks and realizes the truth of what I'm saying. The emotional state he has put himself in while telling me about his impasse is exactly where the character needs to be during the scene.

I thought about this for a long time before I realized that it was because actors don't like to look confused. Who does? Who wants to appear to an audience as if they don't know what they're doing? It makes people look amateurish, and who wants that?

But what's taking place in rehearsal is that in each instance the actor is confusing his own loss of control with that of the character. What I have to impress upon the actor each time it happens is that this loss of control, this confusion, this being really stopped in one's tracks without a clear place to go, is *riveting*. It's a place of pure potential, a place where anything can happen, a wonderfully deep and empty place. I've seen this moment over and over in people's faces when I watch old episodes of *Candid Camera*—the perplexed look, the totally empty space people fall into when they're confronted with outlandish behavior. I laugh at this emptiness far more than I do at most controlled, thought-out comic behavior. When actors have the courage to present us with this open, vulnerable, empty moment it is pure gold. "I don't know who I am, I don't know where I am, and I don't know what I'm doing." It's the essence of the ideas expressed so beautifully in the book *Zen Mind, Beginner's Mind*, by Shunryu Suzuki. He says in the prologue: "In Japan we have the phrase *shoshin* which means beginner's mind. . . . This does not mean a closed mind, but actually an empty mind and a ready mind. If your mind is empty it is always ready for anything; it is open to everything. In the beginner's mind there are many possibilities, in the expert's mind there are few."

When an actor has the courage to really embrace this state, which will occur over and over again during the course of his career, his work will get richer and more interesting.

In the early part of 1997 my then wife, Barbara Dana, who is a fine novelist, called to tell me she was going to try to write a play. She'd bought a script-formatting computer program and didn't know how to use it. Could I help? I tend to like computers, so I told her that if she gave me the program for a while I'd fool with it and see if I could dope it out.

I played with it for a few days until it started to feel comfortable. Just before giving it back, I went over what I had written, looking for formatting problems, and I found to my amazement that I'd written a one-act play, or at least most of one. I had no intention of writing a play. In my life I had no intention of *ever* writing a play, but my unconscious had other ideas.

I spent the next few days trying to decipher what the hell I had written, what the underlying ideas were, and then I spent the next couple of weeks trying to make it coherent, bringing the unconscious ideas into what's left of the organizational side of my brain. When I was pretty satisfied with it I asked my son Tony if, just for fun, he'd come to the house and read it with me. He came over, we ran through it, and it felt good—good enough to give me the confidence to call a producer friend of mine, Julian Schlossberg, and ask if he'd like to see a reading of the play. He said yes, and he arranged for it to take place at a small theater in midtown Manhattan.

We did the reading for about fifty invited friends and got a really positive reaction, after which Julian came running over with Elaine May, whom he'd invited to the reading without telling me.

"I loved it," Elaine said. "I'm going to write a companion piece for me and my daughter Jeannie, and the four of us will do it as an evening." Julian said, "I'll produce it."

Tony and I stammered for a while. I had no specific expectations from the reading; my fantasy was that someone might like it enough to include it in a collection of one-acts, somewhere, sometime, but this train had already left the station. Tony was at a time in his life when he wasn't particularly interested in acting, and I had sworn thirty years earlier that I'd never again set foot on a stage, but we were instantly caught up in the whirlwind and the thing took off almost without our being able to stop it.

Elaine wrote a play for herself and Jeannie. She showed it to Julian, who was very enthusiastic about it but said that the evening also demanded something with Elaine and me. Our names would be in front of the theater, and the audience would be expecting to see us work together. Julian also said that I should direct the evening. No one objected, so I said yes. It seemed daunting, the whole undertaking had a dreamlike quality, but I figured what the hell. Elaine wrote a third one-act play, one that included the four of us, and we were off and running.

The evening, called Power Plays, got terrific reviews, and we settled into The Promenade Theater for a long run, which allowed me to re-examine all of my negative feelings about being onstage from thirty years earlier. I found before terribly long that my feelings hadn't changed a bit, but I bit the bullet and tried to find as much joy in the experience as I could. I was deeply proud of Tony's work, Jeannie's performance was also excellent, but we were all braced for a backlash from the critics over the obvious nepotism. To our immense relief, the critics not only accepted it but applauded it. All four of us got terrific reviews, and the family aspect of the evening became a selling point instead of a liability.

About three months into the run, something happened that began gnawing at me. In the piece I'd written, *Virtual Reality*, Tony started taking longer and longer pauses, slowing down the play, causing the energy to drop, and we were losing laughs. One night after getting offstage I talked to Elaine about it. Elaine watched our play every evening for the entire ten months' run. She has a penetrating analytical mind and a deep investment in everything she's involved in. I asked her if my assessment of what was happening was correct. She said yes, agreeing that Tony was letting a lot of air into the play. "You know what he's doing, don't you?" she asked. I said no. She said, "He's trying to regain some control of the event." That was all she said, but it caused me to take a closer look at what Tony was up against in doing this play.

In the first place he was working with his father, difficult enough for anyone under the best of circumstances. In addition, I had written the play, I had directed it, and to make matters worse, although the play is a comedy, my character browbeats and torments Tony's character. He was carrying a huge load and in my respect for his prodigious craft it never occurred to me, particularly since the reviews were so favorable, that he would be feeling this burden. I immediately felt badly for him and had a new respect for what he was capable of taking on. Still and all, I felt I had to say something. My reticence at dealing with the issue was compounded by the fact that Tony takes criticism almost too much to heart. In all the years from his birth on, I think I've criticized him twice. The first time was when he was about two years old and tried to put a nail in a light socket. I told him as gently as I could that I didn't think it was a good idea. His reaction was so dramatic that I knew I'd better be careful about giving him criticism in the future. He's always been admirably self-governing, so criticism was rarely needed. But I've had a difficult time giving him any kind of correction.

I spent several days trying to find a way of broaching the subject without upsetting him. He'd have to face me—father, author, and director—for every damned performance afterward, and I didn't want to create an additional burden for him. Finally, one night as we were putting on our makeup, I started talking generally about actors who took long pauses. Tony joined me in the discussion, and about five minutes into it he said, "What are you trying to tell me, Dad?" Tony knows me too well for me to waffle, and there was no way out, so I took a deep breath and jumped into it.

"I guess I'm taking a roundabout way of saying you're starting to take longer and longer pauses and I think they're hurting the rhythm of the play. I think it's causing us to lose some laughs." And then I said something I'd never said before, something I'd never even thought about before; I suppose for a second I was in the zone. "But more importantly," I went on, "it's keeping you from the possibility of any self-discovery, which is the greatest joy you can have being onstage—the joy of your own surprise. You'll be a lot happier if you try to throw away the tight control."

Tony sat quietly for a couple of minutes, dabbing on his makeup, while I watched our relationship fly out the window. "That's the end of that," I thought. "He'll give his notice tomorrow and I'll see him again in about five years." He left the dressing room and I didn't see him again until we were both onstage. I waited for his entrance to see what I'd be faced with, and as he came through the door there was instantly a drive to his work that was new. He jumped into the play with a burst of electric energy and kept it up for the full forty minutes of the play. I was forced to hang on to his coattails and keep up with the endless flow of inventive things that were coming through him. It felt like an entirely new experience, as if we'd never done the play before. When the lights went out and we got offstage, we stood there looking at each other and laughed like lunatics. I grabbed him, we hugged, then I held him at arm's length and said, "If anyone told you that you stank tonight, what would you say?" "I'd tell them to go to hell," Tony said, laughing. When you're on, when it's working, when you're in the zone, you don't need anyone to give you accolades. His breakthrough lasted for the rest of the run.

I love working with people with whom I've had some previous experience. But for me, it takes an entire project to completely trust the people I'm working with. I need to experience co-workers throughout the arc of an experience from beginning to end before I can relax, and then the second time it becomes easy. I want to feel that I can touch my scene-partners physically, interrupt them, step on a line if it feels right, or suggest an idea without it becoming personal, and I want them to feel the same way toward me.

For this reason, working with my wife, Suzanne, or any one of my three sons has always been a complete joy. Always. With all the possible problems that could arise, I have never, ever had a problem working with my family. Hard to believe, but true. In a lot of ways, I suppose, this has been a cornerstone of my relationship with my sons, who are all actors, among other things, and it's a source of pride for me that they've never taken issue with my giving them ideas, notes, or suggestions, whether I'm involved in their projects or not. Happily, whatever my faults as a father, this has not been one of them. And I never have difficulty in recommending them for a job if I am absolutely sure that they are right for it.

When I direct, I often sense the tension that arises in producers when they hear me say I want to hire one of my sons. They usually don't know me well enough to realize I would never do that unless I was certain that Adam or Matt or Tony would be absolutely right for the part. But after the fact, producers have always been grateful. Not only because of my sons' talent, but because my working with them saves valuable time. For example, if I'm in a scene with Matt and it isn't gelling, I can say, "Matt, it's Grampa doing one of his lectures," and Matt will immediately know what I'm talking about, the problem is solved, and it's saved a half-hour with an actor who was looking for a way to play a scene.

One of the most poignant moments I've had with any of my sons happened years ago when Adam was at a theater in upstate New York in previews for a play that was headed to Broadway. He called me late one night, after one of the shows, in a mild panic. He said, "Dad, is there any chance you can come up and take a look at this? I think I'm stinking this up and it feels like the play is in serious trouble." Nothing in the world makes me happier than putting on my "Dad suit," so I told him I'd be there the next night to see what was going on.

The next day I drove up to see the play and I sat through an absolutely delightful evening watching Adam fly. He was consistently terrific, funny as hell, and the play worked beautifully. I went backstage with a sense of great pride but also feeling a considerable loss. The person I saw in the play was a fully mature actor with a commanding stage presence, doing really first-rate work. I had no notes, no ideas, no criticism. I just told him he was nuts for feeling insecure, he was terrific in the part, and that the play was great fun. And as I spoke I watched one of my favorite roles of fatherhood fly out the window. In just a couple of hours I had lost my place as a mentor in Adam's life; I was now a colleague. It was a bittersweet moment. The show was called *I Hate Hamlet*, it ran for months, and Adam went on to get a Tony nomination for his performance.

CHAPTER TWELVE

When directing, I learn things about actors that I never notice while I'm acting. For example, in every play I've ever cast I have found myself saying to auditioning actors, "That was very interesting, very good, now try it again without the acting." In every case where I've said this, and there have been literally hundreds of occasions, there has never been an actor who didn't know exactly what I was talking about. When I say it to them, when I tell them to read again and take out the acting, it invariably makes the actor breathe a sigh of relief and smile as if they're saying, "You mean you actually want me to do what I was *trained* to do? What I *enjoy* doing? I can just *play* the part? I don't have to *sell* the part?" I have them go back and do the scene again, and it is invariably looser, more personal, and infinitely more interesting.

We live in a culture where everything is selling. I watch TV and I don't see events, I see people selling me events. The newscasters are not reporting the news, they are dramatizing it, selling it, selling themselves as good re-porters. They're making the news "interesting." They pre-tend they're looking at us when in fact they're watching words on a teleprompter, acting as if they're intimately in-volved with the stories they're reporting, emoting like crazy, performing as though they were actually feeling what they were reading, trying to look as if they were any-where but in the studio.

In interviews, talk show hosts rev us up with hype and personality, offering little or no content, pretending deep concern and intimacy with complete strangers, but mean-while they are busy reading the chalkboard behind the heads of their guests, which is showing them the next question. Actors are selling products they have no feeling for; the political forums are all jazzed up and contain end-less faked fights. We keep watching hundreds of channels waiting for something to actually happen, for someone to be really present. Almost no one ever is. We're so imbued with this onslaught of selling, selling, selling—products and personalities—so bombarded with hype and false ex-citement that I think we forget what a real experience feels like. When we're constantly assaulted in this way we start assuming that what we're seeing is truth. That "this is the way things are." It's the frog-in-hot-water syndrome. We get used to anything, no matter how highly it's ratcheted up, and we begin to believe that since we are *expected* to have an experience we are actually having one. I see it in a great many performances in what are considered our finest movies. I'm not watching living breathing characters; I'm mostly seeing people avoiding real contact with their partners, going for important moments, reaching for awards.

When I directed the film version of *Little Murders*, I was fortunate enough to work with Gordon Willis, one of our greatest cinematographers. In discussing how we were going to put the film together, when something didn't feel right Gordon would say, "No, that's a piece out of the ball." I finally asked him what he meant by that. He said, "When a sequence is working right it should roll in any direction, straight on like a bowling ball with no dents in it." I knew what he meant. We both wanted seamlessness. When I go to a film and come out talking about a performance, or a lighting effect, or the music, or a fancy shot, the movie doesn't work. It works when I don't see any of that. When I'm caught up in the event. When I'm moved. When I'm affected by the entirety. My life has been changed by films I've seen, and I don't want a trip to the theater to be two mindless hours out of my life.

For example, I remember seeing a wonderful performance of Spencer Tracy's that gave me a perspective on the nature of guilt. The film was *State of the Union*. Tracy played an industrialist who had a lot of firebrand and revolutionary political ideas. The character had no trouble expressing them eloquently and passionately, and was ultimately asked to run for president. He did so, and as the film went on, his winning the election started looking more and more possible. Inevitably, his advisers, thinking he could win, asked him to tone down the incendiary aspects of his platform in order to get more votes. Tracy followed their advice, and one of the last scenes in the film is his reading of his final radio address to his wife, played by Katharine Hepburn. He reads the speech to Hepburn, and asks her what she thinks of it. "Do you want me to tell you the truth?" she says. "Yes," Tracy answers. "It's terrible," says Hepburn. "You've sold yourself down the river." She goes on to tell him that in order to win the election he's turned into the same kind of political hack he's denounced his whole life. Tracy listens to her quietly and then has to immediately go on the air and read the speech. He goes up to the mike, rips up the speech, and tells the American people what has happened to him, what he has allowed himself to become—that he'd sold out for a cheap success. The words are contrite and self-disparaging, the kind of speech we see on TV all the time now, where we witness an endless parade of celebrities using the media as the new confession box. Tracy did a version of that, but in his confession his tone was anger at himself. He was enraged at what he had allowed himself to become. There was no obsequiousness, no fawning, no cringing, no asking for forgiveness; he was angry at himself. And in the anger was his power, and I found myself saying, "*He's never going to do it again.* He's over with that behavior." Yes, he admitted his fault, but there was none of that servile submission to guilt that says "This is what I'm like. I'll probably do this again." It was a great life lesson.

Another film that changed me was *My Dinner with Andre*. I remember coming out of the theater embarrassed at what I'd allowed myself to think were the rules of "film making." "It's a visual medium," we are told, over and over again. "The camera tells the story." And then there's *My Dinner with Andre*. We sit in the theater and watch two people at a table in a restaurant *talking* to each other for two hours. Just *talking* and *listening* to each other. And it is riveting. I can barely conceive of the creators and their meetings with producers, trying to sell the film.

I had occasion to spend a day with Arnold Palmer a few years ago. I've never had much feeling for golf, never thought about it much, but after spending a few hours with him I started wondering what it must be like for a professional golfer to be in the middle of an important tournament. I realized that of all the competitive sports, golf might possibly be the hardest under pressure. There's no leeway. If you're a sixteenth of an inch off with your stroke, the ball can be a hundred feet off at the end of the fairway. I wondered about this, and asked him if he ever felt anxious during tournaments, if he felt pressure. "Sure," he admitted. "What do you do when you feel that?" I asked. "I go back to basics," he said easily. Of course. It's what he would have to have said. Keep your eye on the ball. Breathe. One of the greatest golfers in history, and he's not ashamed to go back to the beginning. To start all over again each time he goes out to play. Once again, *Zen Mind, Beginner's Mind*.

Jean Renoir was one of the greatest film directors of all time. His scripts, mostly written by him, were also brilliant. And, on top of that, he was a fine actor. His films make you want to jump onto the screen and join in the fun. There is an effortless ease to all of them, which hides his extraordinary mastery of the medium, and a brilliance with the camera that can be fully appreciated only if you turn off the sound and watch one of his films without the distraction of the story and the performances.

Renoir's first rehearsals consisted of gathering the cast together and reading the script several times with no intent to "act," reading as if it were a laundry list, or the phone book. Intuitively, Renoir understood and had adapted the lesson of *Zen Mind, Beginner's Mind*. This method prevented his actors from making quick and obvious choices about their characters; it prevented them from falling into clichés.

I remember using this method once in a film where an old friend and I were playing the leads. We sat for two days reading the script, devoid of any commitment, of any expression, injecting none of our own ideas or personalities into the material, simply seeing, feeling what the author and his characters were telling us. For the first couple of hours, alone with my friend, I felt tremendous anxiety. Fear, even. Most of me wanted to jump into a safe old place, even though there was absolutely nothing at stake. At any moment I could have done that, but I stayed with the method even though it was new, naked, and unsettling. I think the performance that resulted is one of the best things I ever did.

Our tendency when reading a script for the first time is to tell ourselves we know how to do it. So we dredge up the old formulas and clichés that have gotten us to whatever position we've earned in the industry, making sure that we don't make fools of ourselves or, even worse, get fired, and we breathe a sigh of relief when the first readings are done.

Over and over again, throughout the years, I've seen examples within my craft and, for that matter, in all of life that showed me the necessity of looking through the new eyes of a beginner. The more craft I developed, the more that need grew. In my film work I reached a point where, on occasion, just before beginning a scene, I would force myself to think about other things. Then, on "action," I would throw myself into an event that I had rehearsed for weeks, but in the instant of doing it became brand new, often providing a wonderful surprise. There are actors by the thousands who work on their part and then do it exactly as they prepared it. Sometimes these actors have prodigious gifts. Sometimes they are capable of deeply moving an audience with these gifts. But I wonder, finally, what they end up learning about themselves, what gifts they end up giving themselves. For me, every activity I engage in has to contain the possibility of internal growth; otherwise it ends up as either "making a living" or "passing the time"—two ways of going through life that feel to me

like a living death. I want to know with every passing moment that I am alive, that I am conscious, that with every
breath I take there will be some possibility of growth, of
surprise, and of complete spontaneity.

intermission

Ralph Richardson and John Gielgud, two of the greatest actors of the English theater, worked together a lot. On one of these occasions Geilgud was directing, with Richardson playing the lead role. As rehearsals went on, Geilgud noticed that Richardson was behaving a bit strangely. Richardson was spending a lot of time pacing around, frowning, and talking to himself. Gielgud watched him go through this for a while, then asked him what the problem was. Richardson said, "I don't know what it is. I'm having trouble with the opening scene. With my first entrance. I feel as if the entire part hinges on the way I come through the door for the first time. If I can find my first entrance I think I'll have the whole thing. In fact, I'm quite sure I'll have the whole thing. But I can't find it. Haven't got a clue." Gielgud consoled him, confident that Richardson would find what he needed; he always did.

But as rehearsals went on Richardson got more and more frustrated. More and more preoccupied. His entire concentration seemed to be directed at the problematic first entrance. He tried endless ways of coming through the door. He came in fast, he came in slow, he entered in high spirits, he entered in low spirits, he tried throwing his hat across the room aiming for the hat rack, he tried backing in, he tried creeping in, skipping in, walking in backward and then turning around very quickly; he tried doing a summersault. Nothing worked. "I can't find it," he kept saying. "The first entrance is the whole play for me. The whole character lives in that first entrance."

Gielgud continued to try to make him feel better. Every day at lunch Richardson would leave the table and head for the nearest door to practice his entrance. He opened imaginary doors in the middle of conversations. He watched other people open doors. He dreamed he was opening doors. Weeks went by. The whole cast began to wonder what was happening to their star. Finally, during the last days before the opening, during one of the tech rehearsals, with the two ingénues onstage billing and cooing at each other quietly under the lights and Gielgud in the back of the theater running light cues, Richardson came barreling onstage, makeup half on, hair disheveled, Kleenex hanging out of his collar.

"John!" he shouted into the lights. "John! Are you out there?" "I'm here, Ralph," Gielgud called back hopefully, "What is it?" "I've found it," Richardson said triumphantly. "I've found my entrance. I know how I'm going to do it." "What is it, Ralph?" Gielgud called. "What have you found?" "I'm just going to come in," Richardson said triumphantly. "I'm just going to walk right in." "That sounds marvelous," said Gielgud. "That will be perfect." And that was the end of that.

PART
two

CHAPTER THIRTEEN

Sometime during the '90s I got a call from Susan Scorbate, the dean of Bennington College. We chatted for a while and then she came to the point of her call. She wanted to know if I would give the commencement address for the graduation class that June.

I was shocked. "I don't think it's really appropriate for me to give a commencement address," I said. "Why not?" she asked me. "I got kicked out of Bennington," I told her. "So did I," she answered.

Her comfortable confession put us on common ground, and we talked for a while, the two miscreants. I ended up not wanting to give the commencement address; the idea of writing a speech was appalling to me. But I did feel that I wanted to do something for the college in return for the scholarship they'd given me and which, except for a couple of performances, I had for the most part squandered. She asked if I wanted to teach an acting course, and that didn't appeal to me either, for reasons I didn't understand until years later. I thought for several weeks about what I might want to do instead, and came up with the idea of doing an improvisational workshop. Susan liked the idea and we formulated a ten-day program with thirty-five students, from freshmen to seniors.

It was an imbalanced, cumbersome group with greatly varied levels of proficiency, but what transpired was so exciting and so filled with wonderful scenes that six days into the workshop I thought we had enough material to do a show for the rest of the college. Bennington is a small school and everyone lives on campus, so it was easy to arrange. After another four rehearsal days we put on a two-hour show for the student body using all-original material that the group had created in a little over a week. It was an exciting and revelatory evening.

In the group there were two sweet, bright girls who were not terribly inventive. They got pushed to the side in scene after scene, and when it came time to put on the show they had very little to do. At the end of our last rehearsal, just before the dinner break, an hour and a half before the show was to go on, they came to me and said, "Before we break for dinner can we show you a scene?" "It's too late," I answered. "The show's been set, and there isn't any time to revise it." "We don't want it to be put in the show," they said. "We just want to do it for the group."

How could I say no? I called back the group and we gathered in the audience while the two girls got onstage. They started their scene. It became clear after a couple of minutes that they were playing themselves, and that the scene was about the two of them leaving a rehearsal. As they pretended to put on coats and hats they talked about how much fun they were having in spite of the fact that their work wasn't very good. They mimed leaving the theater and going out in the cold to their car, a Volkswagen, which was now covered with snow. They mimed shoveling the snow off their car, still talking about the workshop, laughing and joking, imitating other people in the group and wishing they had been more inventive. Then they got into the car and it wouldn't start. They laughed at that, and one of them said, "Wouldn't this be a funny scene?" "What do you mean?" the other replied. "Just this," said the first. "The two of us leaving rehearsal, not coming up with anything interesting to do, and then not being able to start the car. Why didn't we think of this when we were in rehearsal? This could have been a good scene." They laughed again and talked about how they would do the scene if the workshop was still going on; then the car started and they mimed driving off to their dorm. The scene was so charming, so real, so filled with love and humor and wonderful Pirandello layers and ironies that it broke all of our hearts, and there was no choice but to include it in the show. Not only include it, but it was so relevant to the spirit of the week that it became the centerpiece for the entire evening.

The workshop at Bennington inspired me enough to want to do more of them. I remembered that a few years earlier I had been approached by The Omega Institute in upstate New York, an organization that offers a huge variety of courses in all kinds of self-exploration. They had asked me if I wanted to do some kind of program there. At the time I was honored by the request, but didn't feel as if I had anything much to offer. Now I thought perhaps I did.

The Bennington experience hadn't felt like an acting workshop. There was something else at play there. It tapped into something broader and deeper. The students were uncovering issues of their own. They were sifting through real problems and touching on real answers. I have over the years been asked to teach acting classes, which I've never wanted to do. There was something about the idea that bored me and turned me off. Doing the improvisation workshop had a different feel. In the week and a half I spent working with the kids at Bennington I'd seen much of the group get out of themselves and fly, do things they didn't know how to do, go to new places and effortlessly get into the zone. If I taught acting classes I could imagine doing it for fifty years and at the end have helped a handful of people learn to fly. But in just ten days at Bennington there were a dozen kids who were aloft, who had discovered that improv could get them into a core part of their "selves." It seemed to be about acting, directing, writing, and self-discovery, all at once, and its implications beyond craft, and its immediate applications, were inescapable.

The Omega people were interested in doing a couple of workshops and we set up two weekend sessions for that summer. It was the beginning of a whole series of workshops that I did there and elsewhere, most of which happened by word of mouth since I had no desire to turn it into a business. No websites, no business cards, no mailing lists. I wanted it to stay fun, and without the pressure of making it "successful." The best part of it for me was that I seemed to be clear of any personal need for it to work, or even for the participants to be happy or fulfilled or to want to recommend it to other people. I didn't care about any of that. I just wanted to see the participants get out of their own way and be truly present onstage. If they did, great; if they didn't, it was their business. I think this attitude was felt by the groups, even though it was never verbalized, and my sense is that this detachment contributed to their being able to cut loose and take chances, and helped create an atmosphere of ease and experimentation and fun.

In setting up the programs I decided that I didn't want to turn the workshops into a series of party games. A lot of improv techniques are, to my way of thinking, overly intellectual, or go in the direction of precious or clever one-upmanship games. I wanted the exercises to be immediate and practical. As the course developed, I found that in general the exercises I assembled were not wildly exciting. I didn't want to be Santa Claus, allowing the groups to fall into the trap of waiting for endless gifts and surprises from the teacher. That's the actor's disease. We're all waiting for the perfect part. For the perfect agent. The perfect play. The perfect scene-partner. Then "*I can finally do some good work.*" I wanted the group to feel that what they brought to the work was going to make the exercises exciting. In addition, I didn't want to audition people for these groups, something that I could have easily gotten away with, but which felt wrong. I could have asked for résumés, I could have asked for essays that gave me a sense of what the applicants thought of themselves, or told me of their needs. I could have auditioned, but in the end I was convinced it wouldn't help me know in any important way who I would be working with.

Sadly, I look at the groups during their first half-hour of work and I can't stop myself from making judgments. "This person is going to whine all weekend, that one is selfish, this one is going to push too hard, that one is never going to do anything worthwhile, this one is auditioning." But by the second day all my initial judgments are out the window.

I am endlessly surprised. I've been auditioning people for plays for forty years and the surprises still come. So I don't audition. In my professional life I have to work with people with a great range of experience, from rank amateurs to professionals, people who have been in the business for fifty years, people who have never been in front of an audience, and there is no knowing where the good work is going to come from. I've seen amateurs occasionally wipe the floor with the professionals. I recently did a film with eight-year-old Abigail Breslin, who was more of a pro than most of the adults I've worked with. You never know. In addition, and more importantly, I want the workshops to be about life, not show business, and in life you never know who you're going to end up having to spend time with. As a result of this attitude there have occasionally been some wildly eccentric participants in the workshops, but they've tended to act as a catalyst and a prod for the rest of the group. They become a way for the others to dig into the work and show some emotional solidarity around the difficult person. It also gives me a great opportunity to test my ability to work with special problems, and I have to do it spontaneously.

I had a guy once decide that he wanted to recite his poetry in his underwear. He stripped down to his briefs, sat a woman onstage in a chair for no purpose that was ever explained, and proceeded for half an hour to read poetry he'd written in the workshop, much of which was about my private parts. The hardest part of the ordeal was finding something positive to say to him afterward. Other people occasionally use their allotted time to audition material they've been working on. I try to discourage this because it has nothing to do with improv, and gets the workshop sidetracked and into performance, but if that's the way they want to use their time it's their business. Fortunately it doesn't happen very often.

CHAPTER FOURTEEN

We watch puppies and kittens at play. They shake sticks between their teeth and growl, they tumble around, falling all over themselves, they grab each other by the neck, they leap at imaginary things; it is when animals are at their most delightful.

It's easy to fall in love with them at this stage of their development. They're cute and cuddly and amusing, at least when they're not ruining our shoes or the furniture. But what we miss is that for the puppies and kittens there's nothing cute about what they're doing. They might be having fun, but more importantly they're learning all the tools and techniques they'll need for life in the wild. The pouncing, the shaking of sticks, the wrestling with each other, the jockeying for position, it's all rehearsal for their survival, and watching them with this in mind we can see that their play is crucial preparation for events that are matters of life and death.

It is similar for us as children. Watch kids as they play Batman or Superwoman or army hero or Olympic athlete or demolition expert or beauty queen or movie star or astronaut. They have no problem jumping into these roles, which are critical for their development. They go at it full tilt, with every ounce of their power and imagination. Nothing is held back and nothing is left out. There is no embarrassment. There is no fear of failure. It's as if their lives depend on it, and to a great extent I think they do.

You don't have to tell kids how to be Batman or Superwoman, how to find belief and emotional commitment; they simply know. It's built into their DNA. Somewhere along the line, however, in a reasonably healthy person, it becomes unnecessary to continue with this kind of play. I don't know exactly when it happens but I would guess it occurs sometime in late childhood, when an adult identity is starting to form. At this time you see embarrassment and self-consciousness creeping into kids' behaviors when they're asked to play a role. For most of us, as we leave childhood, the technique of learning through role-play is no longer a necessity, and becomes an embarrassment instead.

It's my feeling that many people come to the workshops for this reason—they're stuck someplace or they've forgotten how to play. And although for adults this may be socially appropriate, they feel they've lost something important to them. They feel stifled, dried up, and uncreative. I often hear them express this sense by saying that something inside of them is "blocked," as if they have an emotional problem, or they have lost their talent, and there is fear connected to this feeling. But when I hear this I've discovered that very often they've actually gone through some kind of metamorphosis, and haven't recognized it. I try to give them new techniques, exercises that require a sense of abandonment and play, to help them once more *feel* the creative flow that has been lost.

Life is constantly this, whether we like it or not. Change. Going through developmental stages and then growing out of them. For each stage we develop tools and techniques to help us cope, and in each stage we discover a new "me," and then we have to find the tools and techniques that this new "me" needs to work with.

But techniques don't last a lifetime. We become attracted to one when it mirrors our personality or our interests, and when it solves a problem in our life. But we evolve, we change—we get happier, more at peace, or we get more despairing and disillusioned—and as this happens we have to discard the techniques that previously held us together, We thought they would last forever; they don't. We have to discard these life preservers and throw ourselves into the sea again and grab for new ones. Not fun, not easy, but if the purpose of our work is ultimately self-discovery and not just about making a living, it becomes a crucial exploration.

A lot of people, coming to the workshop, hear the term *improvisation* and immediately think of sketch comedy. My initial job is to get them away from this idea, thinking that they have to be smart-asses and clever and inventive for an entire weekend. I can see it as they first come in. They're afraid they're not going to be clever enough, or interesting enough. They're afraid they're going to have to be creative, which is a terrific paradox, because that's the reason they've come. It becomes my job to help them get over this fear as quickly as possible.

So they come in, about twenty of them—writers, lawyers, teachers, psychologists, and people from the theater, many of whom haven't done anything in years. Twenty seems to be the limit. If there were more I wouldn't be able to give them individual attention. We work in a bare room, hopefully well lit; there's no stage, no props, no fancy lighting. All we have are folding chairs.

After we all briefly introduce ourselves, I ask the group to stand up and push back their chairs, and we form a circle. I tell them we're going to play ball. There is no ball. I start bouncing an imaginary tennis ball. I tell them if they follow the instructions, their work for the weekend will be much easier and more comfortable. My instruction for this first exercise is that *I don't want to see anything interesting or anything creative.* They look at me to see if I'm joking, but I'm serious. Immediately I see twenty people breathe a sigh of relief. They've all come to tap into their creativity, the instructor has told them *not* to be "creative," and they breathe a sigh of relief. It's as if their creativity is something that has to be reached for at great cost, a thing outside of their normal abilities, that being creative will mean sticking their necks out, doing something embarrassing. Or that creativity is something for geniuses, for special people, and that being creative turns them into Prometheus, attempting to steal fire from the gods, a dangerous act.

The ball gets thrown around the room. It has to go fast. No time for being clever, for thinking how you want to do it. You have to pay attention to where it's going. If someone takes more than two seconds to throw the ball after receiving it, you can see the "creative vibe" creeping in, the attempt to be interesting. When that happens the person's mind gets taken off the game, off the activity, off the group, and is put back onto himself, and the air immediately goes out of the game for everyone. The energy dries up. In that split second it becomes a personality contest and a competition. To keep that from happening I have to make sure the ball stays in motion. After a minute or two of playing with the imaginary ball, people start laughing. They're having a good time in spite of themselves. Without a pause in the action, we change from a tennis ball to something else, anything that occurs to me, anything that can be thrown—a Ping-Pong ball, a volleyball, a feather, a Frisbee, a squirrel.

If the game stays fast, and people stay out of their heads, within minutes the whole group has loosened up. We begin to know who each of us is, and we're all being effortlessly creative and having a terrific time. Without any self-consciousness. At the end of about ten minutes we stop.

"What was the instruction?" I ask them.

"Not to be interesting," they say. "Not to be creative."

"What happened?" I ask.

"We got creative," they say sheepishly. "We got interesting."

"Why?" I ask.

Once in while someone knows the answer, which is: *It is our nature to be creative. Not being creative is an aberration.*

With that one exercise, most of the rules for the weekend have been laid out. I don't state these rules at this point because I don't want to get the group back into their heads. They've just left their heads for ten minutes and it's important to keep it that way.

The next several exercises are geared toward getting the participants to become aware of themselves as a group, to establish the idea of sharing, of working together for a common purpose. This is rarely taught in acting classes, where I often find a subtle, unstated sense of competition between actors. In classes, as well as in much theater and film work, I often feel the vibes of people being extremely nice to each other in order to hide an underlying jockeying for position. I want to counteract that impulse here.

In the second exercise we become machines. We break into groups of six or seven, and I assign numbers. People go into the playing area in the order of their number, and I give an instruction that remains in place for the remainder of the workshop: Unless they have an idea, something that sparks them, they're not to go into the playing area. I call it the playing area to keep it from being a "stage." I don't want to work on a stage. This workshop is not about performance; it's about self-discovery.

Often people jump into the playing area too soon. This happens either because they just want to be up there having a good time or because they don't want to hang-up the other participants by having them wait until they have an idea. But if you go into the playing area without an idea, you're just on a fishing expedition, hoping for inspiration to strike. And if you're up there waiting for inspiration, it rarely comes. It also puts a damper on other people's energy. The lack of commitment and purpose can be felt, and it drags everything down.

Back to the second exercise. We're going to turn ourselves into a machine. The first person performs a motion that suggests a piece of a machine. It can be real, imaginary, anything. When the second person has a way of fitting into the motion, a way of adding to the machine, he joins the first. And so on, until six or seven people in the group are one machine.

What invariably happens the first time through this exercise is that no one touches anyone else. It's understandable; they're strangers. They don't know each other. After the group has become a machine I ask them to do the exercise again, this time making sure that each person is in some way touching another part of this human machine. The difference is dramatic. The event becomes infinitely more interesting and compelling, and afterward we spend some time discussing why. People grope toward articulating a reason but can rarely state what it is.

I have seen this exercise hundreds of times and I think, first of all, there is no machine in history where the parts don't touch. But this is obvious. The subtle aspect of it, the one that's crucial for our purposes, is that the minute the moving parts of the machine touch each other something dynamic takes place. Our attention to what they're doing becomes more acute, and it's more interesting for the participants as well. Why? I think it's because when the parts are touching, *something can happen.* There is a world of possibility now open that was not present before, when there was no touching. I think this translates to any form of "touch." As machines, in this exercise, physical contact is the only kind of touching possible; machines don't make emotional connection. But there are myriad ways for people to "touch" each other, and I find that just introducing this thought to the group brings that awareness to the mix. We don't have to work on it. No touchy-feely exercises. Just talking about this opens the group to the necessity of really relating to each other, genuinely touching each other, making sure that they see, feel, and affect each other as the workshop goes on.

Once, as I sat watching twenty adults turn themselves into bits and pieces of machines, making strange noises and moving with grotesque, awkward mechanical gestures—all of them lawyers, teachers, psychologists, and actors—I pictured the group at a party, an evening get-together, with all the attendant random events and desultory conversations that go on during these evenings. And I imagined one person jumping up and saying, "Hey, everyone, let's play a game! Let's all turn ourselves into machines! We'll break up into groups and become machines." The likely result of that announcement would be that everyone at the party would exchange alarmed looks, smile politely, and go back to their cocktails.

What's the difference? I wondered.

I came to the conclusion that the difference is that in the workshop, although nothing is stated, each person senses that there's a reason for the exercise—there is *meaning* behind it, an intention—and that meaning and intention will be revealed. But what if there was no meaning behind the exercise? What if I had designed it just to kill time, or I came up with it on the spur of the moment because I was ill-prepared? What if I was just bored?

Still, in the minds of participants, simply trusting the fact that there must be a meaning behind the exercise allows them to jump into it fully, and invest it with their own meaning. And it turns out that *that* jumping in, *that* decision and personal investment of *their* meaning is what actually *gives* the event meaning. Who cares whether it's my meaning or theirs? In fact, who gets to decide what the meaning of something actually is?

I am pretty sure that meaning changes from individual to individual. Take an activity like sweeping a floor or cleaning a kitchen. When you think of those activities you probably think of them as acts of drudgery. No chance of doing something creative with jobs like that. Now picture Charlie Chaplin cleaning a kitchen or sweeping a floor. The possibilities become endless. "Well of course that's different," you answer. "He's a genius." Yes, he is a genius, but what are the contributing factors to his engagement in these activities that turn them into genius?

His decision to turn them into creative activities.

His insistence that there was something creative to be mined, even in the most common activity.

The amount of time he'd spend discovering their creative potential.

He could find it anywhere, and so can we. Perhaps not with all the brilliance and grace that were his particular gifts, but we can do it too.

For me, it all comes down to intention.

For the third exercise we again break up into three groups, and again people enter into the playing area one at a time. In this exercise the participants are asked to be part of a moving tableau. They can speak now, but only to communicate with the others in the playing area, not to us in the audience. It's as if they're now extras in a movie, setting the scene, creating an atmosphere, but not calling a lot of attention to themselves. I suggest a place that conjures up a specific mood, a specific tone—for example, an urban park on a warm spring day. One by one each actor has to fill in the scene. We want to see a variety of activities, and we want to see the space in the playing area used creatively, and we want to maintain the feeling of the place and the day. It requires not only that the players be aware of their own activity and their own life in the playing area but also that they fit it into a whole and make sure they are adding to the event. As with all the exercises, if someone is doing something that gums up the works we go back, fix it, and continue. How does someone gum up the works? By having an activity that is random and can't be pinned down— they're wandering all over the stage doing a half-dozen different things, which keeps the next person from finding a clear space or activity in the playing area. They can gum it up by being redundant and doing the same thing the last person did, or by ignoring the tone of the piece and looking for laughs.

The actors are occasionally thrown by this emphasis on group awareness. My experience over the years has led me to believe that most actors don't read the scripts that are assigned to them. Often, in auditions, they're not even given anything to look at but their own parts, which encourages this myopia. In a well-written piece every part has a function, every character is necessary to the whole. Sometimes the function of the character is obvious, sometimes it has to be searched for, sometimes it just adds to the tone and mood. An actor's exploration becomes much easier if he examines the material from the viewpoint of discovering his function in the piece.

For the fourth exercise we break up mostly into groups of three. This is the only exercise of the weekend in which I ask people to jump right in without a plan. This exercise requires no thinking beforehand. No characters, no set up. It only requires immediacy—the actors solving the problem directly in front of them.

The groups of three are given specific tasks to accomplish: putting up a tent, taking a boa constrictor out of a packing crate and placing it in a glass tank, bringing a piano through a doorway and into a room, hanging a huge picture. All are activities that require shared physical activity, spontaneous planning, and a lot of consensus. It's not about making an interesting scene, it's about accomplishing the physical task. Again, this exercise will fail if people try to be funny or inventive, or embellish. It becomes magical when we see people, still for the most part strangers, struggling to find common ground with imaginary objects and having complicated decisions to make. With this exercise we start to see interesting scenes formed before our eyes, without any attempt to be dramatic or interesting.

T. S. Eliot said that all drama is about man's fall from grace and his redemption. I believe that in its most archetypical form this sweeping concept becomes simply addressing a problem and finding a solution. In this exercise we now see the very beginnings of this idea at play.

It's too soon for people to feel as if they're making statements, but in a small way the sense of drama and event has now been subtly added to the mix. A problem needs to be solved. Sometimes we get people who become anxious about not having a character, not having a fix on the dramatic event of the "scene," not having a strong point of view, and they start to bring a manufactured conflict into play. They decide that they're going to be argumentative or petulant or bossy, and you can smell that it's coming out of some fear that "*nothing is happening. We're not getting laughs.*" It invariably ruins the scene. This is not to say that legitimate conflicts won't arise, but these will be the result of ironing out and sharing the specifics of the imaginary objects and the difficulties of the task at hand. Sometimes the conflict will arise out of seeing who has a more realistic handle on what's happening. These are exciting scenes to watch.

Looking for conflict onstage is always an easy way to manufacture a false sense of comfort for a performer. It can get you some easy laughs, and it can give the audience a vague sense that *something is going to happen*, so actors often like to come into a scene belligerently. My understanding is that Elia Kazan instructed his actors to "look for the fight." I hope this wasn't true. In the first place, I think most people are not looking for fights. I think most people go out of their way to avoid fights. And secondly, it's not an actor's job to go around looking for fights (unless he's specifically playing a belligerent character, or a psychopath). It's an actor's job to explore all the aspects of his character, as outlined and hinted at by the author. Finding the fight might be one aspect, or not. It depends on the play and the author's sensibilities. In the early days of Second City we fell victim to that hostility in scene after scene to such an extent that one day during a rehearsal Paul Sills bellowed out, "I'm sick of this damned hostility! For the next two weeks I don't want to see anything but agreement onstage!" Shocked, we tried to comply, gingerly at first, and then after a couple of days of testing the water we found that there was gold in the instruction. We found there was no way in the world to avoid conflict in a scene where two people had different agendas, or even when two people had the same agenda but different vantage points. And what happened was that in watching people attempt to get along, everything became subtler. We'd have to watch the scenes more carefully and pay attention to the nuances. We'd see all the same tensions displayed, but now instead of yelling and rolling eyes and tapping feet we'd see subtle body language and hear difficult and strained pauses, because the truth of the matter is that in all human dealings, no matter how positive, there are tensions. The scenes got so much better, and the word about this new way of working got out so quickly that there are now whole schools of improvisation that insist that you're not allowed to say "no" on the stage! This, of course, is another form of insanity, because if theater is about human relationships, which is *all* it is, then you have to include "no" in there too. But let's throw in a couple of "yes's" every once in a while, for variety.

Before the fifth exercise I talk about the two tools that participants will be using for the rest of the workshop. These tools are the basis of every good performance they have ever seen or ever will see, and even more importantly, in my opinion, they inform a successful life as well, but we don't talk about that.

The first tool is *intention*, and once understood, the deal is that you never enter the playing area without your character having an intention, a specific job to do, a function to perform. This accomplishes several things. First, it makes it impossible to have stage fright or to be self-conscious. There isn't time. You have something to accomplish. Second, it allows you to be alive without self-judgment. You now have something to do that relates to other people, and making clever jokes or trying to be "interesting" will get in the way of what you are trying to accomplish.

The second tool works in conjunction with the first. The intention you pick should make you feel something. It should give you an *emotional context*, which then becomes the second tool. This emotional context will give you a felt connection to the character you are playing, so that when you go into the scene you won't be entering with an intellectual idea but with the sense of a character. These two tools, used with intuition, are the matrix from which everything you do in the playing area comes alive. It takes time and patience to learn how to sense these two tools at work with each other, how to play with them, and even when you do they won't work all the time, but then that's the problem with creative work. Once we think we have a handle on something, we change, and the change requires a new way of examining the problem.

The sixth exercise goes back to a more intense version of the tableau, and for the first time the two tools, *intention* and the connecting *feeling state* it puts you in, become something to work with. In this exercise we will have six, sometimes eight people working in a scene. They have graduated from being extras in a movie to being supporting players, which means that there can be several conversations going on at the same time, but with no one trying to dominate the scene or take over. (That's the stars' job, and the stars aren't here.) Our settings are, for example, a unisex beauty salon on a busy afternoon, or the kitchen of an expensive restaurant at dinnertime, or the emergency room of a hospital on New Year's Eve—places where a lot of different activities can occur simultaneously and yet still have a common thread. Again, people enter the playing area in the order I've given them, not jumping into the mix until they have something specific to contribute that will not obscure someone else's activity. And it's with this exercise that miracles sometimes occur. If the group is sensitive, and people have their antennae out, these scenes can go on for twenty minutes, often with an extraordinary sense of place and tone, and spontaneously contain complex patterns of movement, levels of motion and flow, that if one had directed them would have taken days of meticulous blocking rehearsals in order to reach.

In this exercise I occasionally just watch the patterns of movement unfolding in front of me, and marvel at the cohesiveness and beauty achieved, without the groups having had one minute of rehearsal. When I check the faces of those watching, they're the faces of kids at Christmas, or on the Fourth of July, marveling at what is in front of them. Two or three, sometimes four conversations are going on at the same time, the entire stage is being used, with movement everywhere, and we can follow every bit of it. We in the audience are able to have intimate relationships with a half-dozen characters simultaneously without becoming confused.

It's the difference that I see between chaos and anarchy. Chaos is beautiful. It's the way nature works, endlessly flowing, changing, all the parts bursting with their own richness, their own individuality, and yet constantly in touch with everything else that's taking place around it. Anarchy is every man for himself, when the individual is not only at the center of the universe but is the *only* center of the universe. The difference between chaos and anarchy is evident immediately.

When there is, within the individual, a consciousness of the group, we are watching fractals at work—actors who have taken on, individually, and in reduced size, the characteristics of the larger experience. It's no longer theater but nature, and it's right here that I often marvel at the shallowness of so much of our theater and films. How little is demanded of us. It's as if most directors and writers are sitting next to us, pushing, pulling, turning our heads, focusing our eyes and demanding what we are to see. "Here, here, look over here!" they call out. "Listen to this! Pay attention to this line, this piece of movement!"

With this exercise all of that changes for me, and I think for most of the others watching, and what is before our eyes is a rich, complex, layered event populated with people mostly without theatrical training who have known each other for about four hours. Watching this exercise changes my sense of how much can be taken in and assimilated by an audience that is not being berated by anyone's unspoken diatribe on "*what's important here.*" I can only attribute this clarity and richness to the unconscious attention that the actors are paying to each other, and to where they are in the playing area—the sense that they are complete individuals and at the same time parts of a whole. If I am watching this exercise and I see that the movement is getting messy, if there's a traffic jam, I know it's because someone has come in with a character that doesn't work. The actor doesn't have a specific action or intention. At this point I'll stop the scene, spend some time with the actor, figure out where his intention was off, and we go back to where we were. And then the scene almost invariably self-corrects, and we're watching fractals at work again. After this extraordinary display of cohesion and freedom, we start tightening the reins. The next big chunk of time gets devoted to two-character scenes with very specific built-in intentions.

I have what I consider to be two main functions during the workshop. The first is to be supportive and not judgmental. To allow people to play. To fail. It's improvisation. It's going to fail sometimes.

My second function is to help people get out of their heads. Their clever place. I can see it when it's happening. The truth of the matter is, everyone can. When it's pointed out to the actors, they know it. And so do their scene-partners. And so do the people who are watching. It's usually experienced by the scene-partners as their own sense of awkwardness or failure, a general discomfort. Those of us who are watching the scene settle into an analytical objectivity, our sense of engagement diminishes, and we, like the person onstage, retreat into our heads.

I also sense it in myself kinetically. My body moves back into my chair. My sense of involvement diminishes. When actors are fully present my whole body moves forward toward the players and the scene. *Something is happening.* When I feel that actors have started "playwriting," working in their heads and not with the people in front of them, I stop and I say gently, hopefully without judgment, "Let's back up." I ask them to tell me about the character and what they are looking for. As they start to describe the character and tell me the thing they are trying to accomplish, they almost invariably relax and start to move effortlessly into the emotional state that they have avoided during the scene. In explaining their intention to me, they drop the performance and make real contact. And as I feel their emotional connection with their character start to take hold, I gently stop them and I tell them to stay emotionally exactly in that place, and we start the scene again. Almost invariably the scene is deeper, more spontaneous, and more connected. I've tried to figure out the psychology of this process, but it's remained mysterious. It seems that as someone is trying to explain the emotional state of the character, it allows room for that state to present itself. Often when people begin a scene, in order to "communicate" they try to rev up the emotions and start selling something they don't yet own, which I think just crystallizes and deadens them, and makes the performance intellectual and self-involved. In explaining it to me, in order to make me understand, they are forced to relate to me, and this seems to give the emotional state a place to freely flow, unimpeded from the unconscious. Whatever the inner mechanism is, it works. It makes the scene come alive for the actors, for their partners, and for the audience.

The improv workshops are themselves improvisations. The nature of the group, its specific identity, its personality, its special abilities and resistances will often necessitate new ways of working. Very often a new exercise comes out of a workshop, sometimes a whole new series of exercises. I never plan for this to happen, it just does.

I did a workshop a year ago in Toronto mostly with alumni of the Second City troupe who lived there. It was an unusually bright and cohesive group of people and we had a three-day session, which for some reason turns out to be the optimum length of time for a workshop. By the third day a deep and comfortable bond had developed between all of us, and in one of the breaks a younger actor came over and asked if we could talk for a few minutes. I said of course, and he told me that he had great trouble being positive onstage. He could play anything negative, but it didn't seem possible for him to portray anything joyous. He asked me if I had any advice, and I immediately had a thought. "Can we talk about this in the group? Would you be comfortable with that?" He said sure, so we went back and I said, "Sean has trouble being positive onstage. Let's create a situation where he's *got* to be positive." I told Sean to leave the room for a minute. When he'd gone I said, "Let's throw a surprise birthday party for him. When he comes back in the room, shower him with gifts and praise and we'll see what happens."

I found Sean, told him to come into the room, and the entire group, all twenty of them, jumped into immediate action. They sang "Happy Birthday," they showered him with gifts, they plied him with his favorite food, they sang his praises and within a few minutes Sean had no choice but to lighten up. Within another few minutes he was beaming, and the mission that the rest of the group had taken on, the action that they'd chosen, was working like a charm. The joy was infectious. It ran through all of us, and Sean had an experience onstage he'd never had before in his life.

Everyone sat back down, but they were all fired up. "Does anyone else want to try something?" I asked. Greg, another young man in the group, raised his hand. "I have trouble taking charge onstage," he said. "I can't take on any authority. I'd like to work on that." "Let's do it," I said. "We're in Detroit, you're the foreman in an automobile plant."

With no discussion, no time for thought or preparation, there was an assembly line in front of me. There were five guys working on the line and a chorus of people acting as cars in front of them. It was like magic. The guys on the line were all goofing off and it was up to Greg to whip the operation into shape. Within minutes he was running the plant, barking orders, pushing people around, telling everyone what to do; it was again an experience he'd never had before.

Other hands went up. A young woman said she'd wanted to be a ballerina. She'd had an accident and could no longer dance; it was a part of her life she felt she'd never resolved. We jumped into action. We took her backstage to her dressing room, immediately after her debut as prima ballerina at the Met. We surrounded her with reporters, with fans, her family, the other dancers, all praising her to the skies and she basked in glory.

The afternoon went on like that, and I spent most of it crying tears of joy at the extraordinary degree of love and cooperation that everyone showered on each other. It was a glorious day.

CHAPTER FIFTEEN

I live in New Mexico and was asked recently if I would work with some of the Native American youth, out of the Pueblos, a lot of whom are floundering and lost. For reasons I've never understood I've had a feeling of connection with this culture my whole life, and I was delighted to have the opportunity to work with them and perhaps get closer to them. My wife Suzanne and I agreed to do a one-day workshop at The Institute for American Indian Arts, a local school that's geared to meet the needs of the Native American population of the state.

Normally I plan my workshops for two or three days, with two seeming to be the minimal time that anything transformative can take place, but they wanted to do it quickly and I agreed to one day. I didn't know what could be accomplished in that short a time, but I thought we'd give it a try.

Suzanne and I showed up at nine; people started drifting in about nine-thirty. And we learned our first lesson about the culture: Punctuality is not a trait that belongs to these people who are, I suppose, still governed to some extent by the time sense of their ancestors, the sun being the gauge of where one should be and when.

Around ten A.M. things started to come together. As our session began there was an easy compliance with the exercises, but no real sense of abandon or exploration. Not much joy. I felt more like an employer than a workshop leader. I kept augmenting the exercises, trying to loosen things up—nothing worked. At the end of each exercise I asked if there were any questions, any comments. None came.

By twelve-thirty only one scene had emerged with any element of personal investment. It was a simple transaction scene. I use this exercise to introduce the idea of tasks and objectives. The setting given to the actors was a pawnshop. The young man who was assigned to come into the shop came in with a necklace to pawn. He made it clear, not by anything particular that he said, but by the gentle, loving way he handled the necklace, that the object had been in his family for generations, that he cared for it deeply, and that he was having trouble parting with it. The pawnshop owner was a tall beautiful Inuit woman who decided to play the role as someone who was generous and loving. It became clear as the scene went on that although she had feelings for the young man's situation, the necklace was not an object she could use. She told him finally that she could give him enough money to scrape by for a while, and offered him the promise that she would keep the necklace hidden away for a longer period than usual in order to prevent anyone from buying it.

The scene was very subtle, filled with real feeling for the necklace, and a lot of pain. No other scene had much of anything personal in it. When we broke for lunch I asked that each participant come back with something that moved them, something they felt particularly happy about, or sad, or angry. Something that made them laugh or cry. Anything they felt strongly enough about that could be the basis for a scene.

When we returned I asked the group what they'd come up with. No show of hands. Does anyone have anything they want to turn into a scene? Something that moves them? Nothing. Finally a woman who was one of the instructors in the college said, "I have something that I'd like to work on, something that I feel passionate about." "What is it?" I asked. "Runaway children," she said. "Fine," I said. "Let's turn those feelings into a scene."

She decided she'd like to do something about a runaway son returning home. A young man raised his hand. "I'll be the son," he said. Brad was his name, a broad-shouldered student at the school with long black hair and glasses. "What made you come home?" I asked. He had no immediate answer so we decided that a good element for the scene would be to have two social workers bringing him home to find out the lay of the land between the boy and his mother. Two students volunteered to be the social workers. I told them to stay in the scene until it became clear that what was taking place at home seemed safe. They nodded, left the stage area, and without any preparation the scene began.

The social workers knocked on the door, the mother let them in, and there was her son whom she hadn't seen in six months. The social workers explained to the mother where the son had been found, and that he expressed some desire to return home. The reunion was tense and uncomfortable; the two students playing the social workers watched the interaction like hawks, waiting to see what happened between the mother and her son, which would clarify what their function in the scene would be. Brad was sullen and monosyllabic, refusing to give anything but the most minimal responses to his mother and the social workers, but it became clear after a while that he wanted to stay home, and they left. The mother wanted to know if he would go back to school, he said he would try it out. She also said that her boyfriend had gone away and that the two of them would be a family again. Brad remained sullen and uncommunicative and deeply unhappy.

After about ten minutes I ended the scene. This is one of my roles in the workshops. When I feel that the energy has played out of an event, or if it comes to a natural conclusion, I cut it. I feel it's important for the actors to stay engaged in the moment rather than worrying about where a scene is headed. I can tell when actors are "playwriting" or shaping something, rather than connecting, and when they begin doing that it takes the fire and immediacy out of the work—for the actors, for their partners, and also for anyone watching.

After the scene with mother and son ended, there was a long heavy silence in the group. Each moment in the scene had been true and fully realized, but the event was filled with despair and painful to watch. We sat in silence for a while, drinking in the sadness of what we'd witnessed. I couldn't bear ending the workshop on that note, and I found myself saying, "What can we do for this boy? Where can we take him? Is there anyone in the world he can talk to? What's next for him?" I wasn't comfortable leaving either him or the class in this state. Brad thought he could talk to one of his friends. That didn't make me comfortable. I was concerned that the scene would turn into a joint complaint and become another downer, so I asked the group for a different idea. "He could talk to his grandmother," Brad said. "Okay," I said. "Who's going to be the grandmother?" The woman who'd played the pawnshop owner that morning raised her hand. "I'll be the grandmother," she said. She got onstage with Brad and they jumped into the scene. It was somewhat more comfortable than the last one; Brad clearly loved his grandmother and she him, but the advice she gave wasn't sitting well with him. She asked if he was going to stay home, he didn't know. She told him to speak to his mother about what was troubling him, he wouldn't agree to do it.

The scene, although less tense than the first one, reached another dead end, and I faded out with the two of them in a loving impasse. Again there was this brooding silence and sadness in the group, and again I found myself asking, "Where do we take him now? Where can he go? What can we do for him?" I wasn't going to end the day on this note. Fidel, the man who'd arranged the workshop and brought us to the college, called out, "We don't want any Hollywood endings!"

"I don't want any Hollywood endings either," I said. "But isn't there something between a commercial lie and this terrible impasse? Isn't there some way to open him up? To give him a future of some kind? Some hope?"

There's a technique in dream analysis that I learned a few years ago when I was doing some work in that area, studying with a wonderful teacher and friend, Anita Hall. In one session I presented her with an unpleasant dream fragment that trailed off into a negative limbo. "How would you end the dream?" Anita asked. "It didn't end," I said. "It just trailed off." "End it," she said. Her direction confused me. I had always thought that dreams were impenetrable, as if they were some kind of event coming from another realm. What she was asking seemed kind of sacrilegious, but I tried it anyway. Not wanting to veer too far from the original material, I ended the dream in a dark tone, in keeping with the substance of what I had dreamt. "Does that ending make you happy?" Anita asked. "Not really," I said, "but it seems to be what the dream was heading toward." "Why don't you head it in a direction that makes you happy?"

Her request felt strange and improper, as if she wanted me to tamper with the work of an important writer. But I tried what she said. I gave the dream a happy ending. It was shocking, as if I'd broken some unspoken and archaic law. It was the first indication I had that we don't have to be enslaved by our dreams, that we can direct them, re-shape them, and even eventually, by doing so, change the substance of our unconscious minds.

I began reworking my dreams wholesale, giving them endings that were in keeping with what I wanted consciously for myself. If a dream was frightening or depressing, I fixed it. I ended it in a way that made me happy or fulfilled. I wanted the same thing now in the workshop. That doesn't mean I'm not willing to allow people their pain, or that I'm asking people in the workshops to not share things publicly, moments that, if shared, might mean the release from some private hell. But there's a difference between presenting a picture of a painful past and projecting it into the future, telling us that this is the way things are going to be, the way they *must* be. It's easy to feel the difference. In the first instance you will feel compassion. Empathy. In the second instance you will just be depressed. I don't like to be depressed. What I wanted now, in this series of scenes, was for the group to experience the difference. I hoped that if I badgered them a bit more they might wrench themselves out of this collective bad dream, but there was still resistance.

I jumped into the work area. "Look," I said, "what goes on in here is make-believe. It doesn't have to be a literal representation of our walking-around lives. In this arena we can do anything we want. We can make life anything we imagine. We can create myths, legends, comedies, tragedies; we can dance, tell jokes, sing songs. Why can't we imagine some step for this kid that can help to take him out of his pain and to some slightly better place? Is that too much to reach for?" They sat silently for a while. "I could be his father," Fidel said. Brad liked that idea.

"Where is he?" I asked. "Where does the scene take place?"

"The father's dead," Fidel said. "He's coming to his son as a spirit." "I'll be asleep," Brad offered, and jumped into the scene. He lay down on his back in the playing area. Fidel came up to him slowly and crouched by his head. He began speaking, and what came out of his mouth for the next ten minutes could have been written word for word by one of our great playwrights. Every single word was un-self-conscious poetry.

"I'm coming to you to apologize, my son," Fidel said. "When you were born I was so proud, so proud of having a son, of being a father, that I went out and celebrated. The celebration went on too long. I got drunk with my friends and coming back to you and your mother I smashed the car into a tree and killed myself, so you and I have never met. We've never spent a moment's time with each other. But I have come back to tell you that I have always known that you were *special*. That you had something important and beautiful to do in this world. And I also came back to tell you that I love you."

At this moment Brad slowly came awake. He slowly sat up and turned and saw his father for the first time in his life. He looked into the spirit face of his father. Slowly he reached out his hand to touch his father's hand, and as they touched I cut the scene. I had an instinct that what would transpire would be either talky or maudlin, so I cut it. "Where can we go now?" I asked. "What's the next scene?" "He can go back to his grandmother's," Brad said. He was starting to become filled with energy. "He needs to tell her about this." "Okay," I answered.

The woman who played the grandmother came back on-stage. Immediately they went into the next scene, and this time there was some enthusiasm from Brad. A sense of wonder at what had just taken place between him and his father. The grandmother, too, was excited by Brad's account of his meeting with his father. Both treated his dream as if it had really been a real event, and a significant one. The grandmother encouraged Brad to now go back to his mother.

I cut the scene and the woman playing Brad's mother came back onstage. The grandmother left. Brad came into the house with a newfound power. He had things to tell his mother now with the courage that he'd found by bonding with his father. The mother sensed this and tried to circumvent what Brad was leading up to, but he didn't allow it. He forced his mother to listen to him, to hear things about her old boyfriend that she didn't want to hear. "He raped me," Brad said. "Not once but continuously, for four years." The mother shut her ears. She denied and denied it, but Brad forced her to accept the truth of what he was saying, and that somewhere, despite her denials, she knew. The scene ended again in pain and despair.

"Where do we go now?" I asked again. By this time the group knew that I wasn't going to let go until the boy was somehow redeemed and given a life. A woman in the back said, "I have an idea." "What is it?" I asked. "Can I just tell Brad about it?" "Sure," I said. She talked privately with Brad for a moment and jumped into the scene. She pulled up a chair and was instantly in a car, driving down a road. Brad came onstage as a hitchhiker. The woman picked him up and after he settled himself in the car she asked him where he was going.

"Santa Fe," Brad said.

"What are you going there for?" the woman asked amiably. "It's my home," said Brad. "School's out and I'm going back to be with my mother."

"Oh, that's nice," said the woman. "Where are you in school?"

"I'm ending my senior year," Brad said. "Then I'm going to college."

"What are you going to be studying?" the woman asked.

"Astrophysics," Brad said.

"That's an unusual thing for an Indian to be going into."

"I'm joking," said Brad easily. "I'm probably going to be a teacher."

They chatted pleasantly for a few minutes, the woman rambling on happily about her plans for the weekend, and

I slowly faded out on the scene. Brad had given himself a life. He was back in school, somehow reconciled with his mother, and envisioning a future for himself. The resolution was subtle, upbeat, and very moving. Realistic, plausible, and positive without a Hollywood ending. The entire event had taken over an hour and every moment in it was true and honest and perfectly placed. It felt like a brilliantly conceived play that had been rehearsed for a month and had already received rave reviews. The workshop was over and I breathed a sigh of relief.

I found out the next day from Fidel that the people in the play had called each other that night and were planning to get together and try to write a transcript of what they had just created. They had a vague plan to piece it together and perform it around New Mexico. "We're probably going to change the last scene," Fidel said. I didn't press the point. I loved the way it had ended. I thought it had been quietly revelatory, but it wasn't my piece. I found out a few weeks later that they had abandoned the project. It had been too much of an ordeal.

As I went over the experience in the following weeks, and got past my own intense emotional reaction to material this difficult, I could not help but believe that their creating it, sharing it, putting it out there for each other in such a communal and embracing way had a lasting, positive effect for all those who were involved.

CHAPTER SIXTEEN

So Suzanne and I are in Hawaii, doing a week-long workshop. There are only about nine people in the group, and as a result the work is pretty concentrated, pretty intense. Among us is a sweet, gentle Japanese-American woman in her early forties named Karen. She's a psychologist, quite serious, attentive, and intelligent but also reserved, and her work is not terribly inspired. It's as if she's trying to go unnoticed.

This is a rather odd syndrome for someone taking an improvisation workshop, but it often crops up, and when it does I begin to see it as early as the first exercise, the imaginary-ball-throwing game. Invariably, there are three or four people who never get the ball thrown to them; they seem to have negative magnetism. It's fascinating. During the many times we've played this game Suzanne and I have tried to find some common thread that runs through these people. What could it be about them that seems to repel the ball?

We watch carefully. They are not particularly unattrac-
tive, imposing, or unfriendly looking. They are not actively
hostile. It's too early in the experience for any of the others to
have developed hostility toward them because at this point in
the workshops everyone is too busy trying to make a good
impression. So it can't be an intentional shutout, and there's
nothing in their demeanor that is particularly off-putting,
but I do sense a kind of cloud around them, a haze that ren-
ders them somehow invisible. Perhaps they've come here because they're aware of their invisibility and are trying to find a
way to break out of it. I don't know. Suzanne and I have finally come to the conclusion that they must be uncon-
sciously projecting a quality that says, "I don't belong here.
I'll never be part of the group; no one will ever throw the ball
to me." We can't figure out what else it could be. But when
we see this taking place Suzanne and I both make an effort to
include these people in the game. If no one else throws the
ball to them, we do, and at this stage of the workshop I don't
feel badly about forcing the issue a little. Later on when
people are designing their own scenes, and picking the people
they want, the issue comes up again. Some people don't get
chosen, others end up being in half a dozen scenes, and at
this point I have decided to keep out of it. Perhaps there is a
better approach to this issue but I haven't found it. Yet.

But back to Hawaii. On the evening of the third day,
at the end of the session, Karen comes over to Suzanne and
they walk up the hill to dinner. People often confide in Suzanne when they're shy about approaching me. Perhaps

they feel they don't want to burden me, perhaps they're afraid of what they'll hear, I don't know. With Suzanne they know they'll get a sympathetic ear.

"I'm frustrated," she says to Suzanne. "Why?" Suzanne asks her. "I want to be funny. I want to do something funny," says Karen. "Well, it's probably better not to force the issue," Suzanne replies. "You know the workshop isn't about being funny, it's about being spontaneous and present in the moment. All of your work is very present, very accessible. Some of the best scenes all week have been very serious. You've seen that yourself."

"Well," says Karen, "I want to be funny."

Suzanne commiserates, trying to make her feel better, but it doesn't help, and Karen goes back to her cabin frustrated and unhappy.

The next day we're doing scenes where the instruction is that each participant has to be a leader of some kind. Karen has decided that she is going to lead a group therapy session. It's a bit of a stretch, but it's in the ballpark, so she gets ready. She sets up a group of chairs in a semicircle and asks for a volunteer to be the patient. A woman named Beth says she'll do it, and the scene begins.

"*The* patient? One patient in a group therapy scene?" I ask myself. "How's she going to handle this?"

Beth knocks on an imaginary door. Karen says, "Come in."

Beth comes in. Karen says, "Hello, and welcome. I am Dr. Ping-Pong. Are you here for the group therapy?" Beth says she is and introduces herself. Karen says, "Well, nobody else is here yet, so we'll just wait for the rest of the group to come."

Karen has turned herself into an immigrant Chinese woman with only a moderate grasp of English; she is serious, gentle, and meticulous. She points to a chair, Beth sits. Karen sits. They remain there in silence for what feels like half an hour.

Finally Karen says, "Well, it looks like no one else is coming so we will begin the session." She motions for Beth to begin and Beth starts to tell Karen her problems.

"No, not yet," says Karen. "First you have to introduce yourself to everyone." Beth looks around the room. "There's no one here," she says. "Well, this is group therapy, and we have to do it the right way," says Karen. She motions to the room. Beth introduces herself to the imaginary people and then jumps right in, telling Karen her problems.

"Not yet," Karen says again. "You have to let everyone else introduce themselves." She motions to the circle of chairs and waits perplexed but calm, while the nonexistent patients introduce themselves. Beth is starting to look slightly crazed. After all the patients have introduced themselves, Karen says, "Well, Beth, since you are the new one, why don't you tell us what brought you here."

Beth tells us her issues. Karen listens attentively and then says, "Would anyone in the group like to comment?" She listens attentively to the comments of the nonexistent group, occasionally nodding and agreeing, Beth looking more and more uncomfortable.

By this time, all of us watching the scene are in hysterics. Beth is playing her part with a deadly seriousness, and Karen's performance of the therapist is brilliant. Her work is quiet and careful and patient. And funny, from a very unusual place—I can't recall any other comedy performance that came from this specific place. The scene goes on until we're all coughing and choking with laughter, and I finally yell "cut" because we're in too much pain to watch anymore.

That evening Karen told us she called her husband, who was another therapist. "Do you think I'm funny?" She asked him.

"No!" he said without hesitation.

"I made everyone in the group laugh today!" Karen said proudly.

And for the next two days she played Ping-Pong in every scene. No matter what was called for, she found a way to fit Ping-Pong into the mix.

CHAPTER SEVENTEEN

In another workshop, at The Crossing in Austin, Texas, a woman named Billie gets up to do a scene. It is toward the end of the weekend, during the free-play section, where people can do scenes about anything they want. My only requirement is that they choose something they have a strong feeling about. It can be funny, sad, whimsical, something from their life or imaginary—I don't care as long as it comes out of a strong personal impulse.

Billie needs to vent. This workshop has twenty participants, eighteen of them women, which has given this weekend a feminist cast, and an aggressive one at that. There are no raised clenched fists, no obvious men-bashings, no shouts of "Sisterhood Is Powerful," but you can feel it in the room. Each workshop develops its own particular personality, and, who knows why, this one verges on the militant.

Billie's scene takes her to a restaurant where she is meeting her ex-husband to ask him for more child support. Although it isn't stated, it seems clear that she is trying to work out something from her own life. She talks briefly with the man playing her ex and the scene begins. Billie decides to be late for the lunch, which puts her immediately on the defensive and in an apologetic frame of mind. The ex, it becomes instantly clear, is a son-of-a-bitch who hates Billie. He knows why she is there and is intractable and abusive. Billie takes it and takes it, and as the scene progresses she becomes more and more powerless as her entreaties about needing money fall on deaf ears. Billie begins to cry and beg, which makes her ex even more abusive.

After about ten minutes, Billie, in a fit of despair and rage, pulls a pistol out of her purse and shoots her ex pointblank in the face. He falls off his chair, dead, and the workshop breaks into wild applause. I let it die down, and ask, "What's the next scene?"

We haven't played this game in this workshop before, so it takes a minute for Billie and the group to catch on. The event isn't over. We don't go far afield, deciding to simply continue with what would probably take place in the restaurant immediately afterward. Billie goes back to the table, and we get a restaurant manager to surreptitiously call the police.

Billie is sitting, gun in hand, stunned, but filled with relief and a quiet sense of triumph. Two officers quickly show up, talk to the restaurant manager, and then quietly and carefully approach Billie, who has jumped right back into her role. Her feeling of triumph is short-lived under their questioning. They gingerly demand the gun, which she reluctantly gives them. "You'll have to come with us," says one of the cops. "Why?" Billie asks. "You just shot and killed someone in front of twenty witnesses," he answers.

Billie is confused, and her sense of righteous indignation starts to flag when she is handcuffed and questioned. She tries to explain the frustrating and abusive relationship with her ex to the cops, who are of course disinterested, and they drag her off to jail. They put her in a cell, lock it, and leave. Billie, now coming down from her high, is in a state of shock and confusion. She's gone from being a heroine to a jailbird in a couple of minutes.

"What's the next scene?"

Billie is a fine actress and is caught up in her emotional state, so she is unable to help in structuring the next step. I suggest that we just take it to the next logical place, which is a visit from her teenage daughter. Billie is okay with that, and a young woman volunteers to play the girl. Billie settles herself in her cell again and the daughter is escorted in. Billie rushes over to hug her, to get some comfort; the daughter freezes.

"What's wrong?" Billie asks.

"What's wrong?" the daughter says incredulously. "You killed my father!" The scene progresses for a while with Billie trying to explain why she did what she did, and although the daughter has some understanding of Billie's pain and frustration, the daughter forcefully lets Billie know that she is now without a father and a mother. The daughter then exits, having left Billie completely unable to make any real connection with her.

"Where do we go next?" I ask. "What's the next scene?" Billie still can't wrap herself around what's happening, so I say, "Well, why don't we get your lawyer in here. Let's go into your first meeting with your lawyer."

Billie is okay with that idea and nods her assent. We give her a few moments to get used to her jail cell; then a woman who volunteers to play her lawyer comes in, escorted by a guard. The guard leaves, and Billie, excited and hopeful at seeing her lawyer, asks what lies ahead. What the possibilities are before her. "Where are we? What are we going to do?" she wants to know.

The lawyer is stern, tough, even unfriendly. There has been no time for the woman to work on her part or decide what she is going to do, but in two seconds she is a completely realized character. "What's going to happen?" she says. "You shot and killed a defenseless man in front of twenty witnesses. What do you think is going to happen?" Billie tries to explain the extraordinary level of frustration that she'd been feeling, the years of abuse she has suffered at the hands of this man, but the lawyer tells her no one is going to care. "This is Texas," she says. "If you're lucky you'll get off with a life sentence." The lawyer gives her a couple of pieces of information and then leaves.

Billie is left alone in a state of real-life despair and confusion. Her sense of triumph and vindication has collapsed. The fantasy of her ex's death being a happy, final resolution has gone up in smoke.

"What's the next scene?"

We decide to jump forward a couple of years. Billie is now in prison, serving a life sentence. The scene is the prison yard, exercise time. Billie is just sitting. Waiting. Her life as she knew it is over. I send in a woman, Joanie Mercer, to be a friend. In about two seconds Joanie completely transforms herself. She has become an elderly Southern woman, and it is immediately evident that she's been in the prison for a long, long time, although we never find out why. It's also clear that she is a thoughtful and dignified person.

She goes and sits next to Billie, who is now lost and resigned. After a short greeting and some pleasantries, the old woman says, "Billie, I have a couple of things to tell you." Billie looks at her. The old woman goes on: "Billie, I'm dying. It's something I've known for a while, but they confirmed it for me in the infirmary just now. I don't have much more time to be with you, and I wanted to tell you right off."

Billie begins to cry and holds her friend. The old woman consoles her, completely devoid of concern for her own condition. When Billie is able to control herself, the woman says, "There's something else I have to tell you." Billie asks her what it is. The old woman says, "You know, I have heard you say over and over again in the time I've known you that you want respect. That you need respect. I have heard you talk about that so often that I went to the library and I looked up what that word means. And do you know what I found out? The word means to re-look at something. To re-examine something. And my guess is that it means you have to re-examine yourself. Re-examine something about yourself. And I thought it might be something that you might want to consider."

Once again Billie starts to cry, and I let the scene go on for about a half-minute, with the two women holding each other, warming each other.

"What's the next scene?"

The event isn't over yet. It still needs something. I gingerly ask Billie how she feels about going back to the restaurant, back to the very first scene with her ex-husband, and doing it over again. She says okay. She takes a minute to collect herself and goes back to the restaurant. Her ex has placed himself in the same position he was in when they first met. He's adopted the same pose and has the same intractable attitude. Once again Billie rushes in, late, but there's a new, self-sufficient air about her. Her bearing is different. She doesn't apologize for being late. She sits down and after a rather formal exchange of "how-are-you's" she states her case.

Her ex begins to abuse her as he had done in the first scene. She tells him crisply and politely to stop doing it; she has no intention of pursuing the relationship in any way, and wants only an answer to her one question. "I am having money difficulties. Will you give me more child support?" The ex says no and is about to go into his rant, continuing his abuse, but Billie gets up and, with all of her dignity intact, cuts him off, thanks him for his time, and leaves the restaurant.

The applause was deafening. Billie seemed to be in a state of mild shock for the rest of the day. In an e-mail about a month later she wrote that the experience was life-changing. Joanie told me afterward she had no idea where her character came from, that it was a person completely out of her conscious frame of reference.

CHAPTER EIGHTEEN

The last exercises over, there is a bonding that takes place that seems out of proportion to the scant two or three days we've spent together. Hugs, tears, exchanges of phone numbers, e-mail addresses, lots of picture taking. There's been so much deep revealing done with such abandon, so much trust, so many funny and tearful moments, so many forms of theater found effortlessly as a result of honesty and need, never to impress.

We often sit around and talk informally for a while. Nobody wants to go home. And I get asked this question after almost every workshop.

"How do we bring this back to the real world?"

The first time I heard it I was shocked and started laughing. "What was all of this?" I said. "What was going on the past two days? Was this fake? Was this all an imaginary experience? Do you think I did it for the money? That I put on a performance? Do you think that the other twenty people here were busy trying to con you into some vision of themselves? This *is* the real world! It's as real as anything you've ever experienced!"

But after hearing the same question a number of times I began to realize that what's really behind it is the sense that these people, for a few days, had found a place they enjoyed, where they were accepted and allowed to express themselves openly, without reservation, with a group who gave them nothing but support and encouragement in return. *That's* what they wanted to bring back into the "real world."

Why did it happen? Why could they do that, here? I know some of the reasons, but not all of them. I know that part of their ease comes from encouragement, which allows them to be unafraid and completely present and in the moment, here and now, with no expectations other than their own unfolding. If something is to come out of the experience it will come out of devotion to what is taking place right now. I believe this fervently, both in life and in a workshop: that if this present moment is lived whole-heartedly and meticulously, the future will take care of itself.

I also know that if a performance was going to come out of the experience, if we were going to put on a show, it would all change. People would start watching themselves, protecting their turf. Hidden hopes and dreams for an imaginary future would take hold and infect the atmosphere.

So what I tell people now, after insisting that there has been not one moment of faking, or trying to impress anyone, on my part, or Suzanne's, that these few days have been as real as anything they've ever experienced—what I tell them now is that they are under an *obligation* to bring whatever was alive for them in this room—the sense of freedom and flight they've touched upon here, and which has become embedded in their consciousness—that they bring this back into the world, into their "real" lives, and that it finally inform every part of their existence.

I don't know what each of them has experienced in the last few days. It's different for each person. Often we hear from people who seemed to have been hiding for the weekend, who seemed to unfold not at all, people we felt we haven't touched, and we'll get a letter saying their lives have been changed dramatically. For each it's a kind of re-finding of something lost, or perhaps a letting go of something that was holding them back, and I guess that can only come from having been in a place where such self-exploration has been allowed and encouraged.

I'm at a point in my own growth where I can say that I don't really care if the workshops work or not, or even if I ever do another. And I think that this letting go on my part—not needing the workshops to be "good," not needing or seeking approval, not needing to find my own identity or validation through them—this can only be good for me and for the workshop participants as well. If I could not let go of my own needs, a tension would be created inside me that would infect everything about the weekends. Whether visible or not, it would be felt. But that seems not to be the case. I don't pick up from people that they've experienced anything but freedom and joy. That's what their question alludes to, so now it's their *duty*, each of them, to insist that this place of openness and connection stay alive within them, and then, to the best of their ability, help create a similar place for everyone they encounter.

We're all sensitive to energies. Mostly we ignore these subtle feelings, push them into the background. But we come home after work and we can sense if a loved one is in a bad mood, or has had a hard day. They can be in the next room, we still sense it. We walk into a meeting that doesn't have a good feeling or a good atmosphere and if we have any degree of consciousness we say, "Uh-oh, bad stuff going on here," and we shut down, or try to remove ourselves from the negativity. But what we forget is that the minute we walk into an environment we become part of it. If it's negative, we become a part of that negativity. The most creative way of dealing with it is to recognize it and then commit ourselves to changing it. It can be done. It takes energy and imagination, but it can be done.

Once or twice in a workshop someone has yelled out, "This is turning into a lot of psychodrama!" The first time I heard this I was completely thrown. I didn't know how to respond. After a couple of hours of doing the exercises, everyone knows I have no interest in having anyone learn how to audition, or be better actors. Frankly, I don't give a damn if anyone in the group ever performs again. Acting is nothing more than a metaphor for life, and a pretty transparent one at that. Theater is supposed to be an art form, but most of the time it's just life up there. In the first part of a theatrical event, the playwright shows us the rules he believes life is governed by, and then he goes about attempting to prove his theories, and he does it simply by showing us human behavior. It's rarely much of an abstraction. Trying to analyze a piece apart from human psychology is nuts. This is why I get tongue-tied when I'm accused of conducting psychodrama workshops.

The second time someone yelled, "This is psychodrama!" another voice yelled back, "*Everything* is psychodrama!" And I realized this was the answer I was groping for. In the workshops, working on one's psychological issues happens almost by accident. It's usually a by-product of having fun, but the thumb-print of our unconscious is always present, as it was for me in the early days of Second City when I thought I was playing this great variety of characters, each one a million miles away from me and my psychology. I wanted nothing more than to hide behind my characters, but they were all me. When I sense someone is avoiding something in a scene, when I push people into examining what's going on, when I prod the person into looking for whatever is stopping the flow, they are never asked to examine their past, their painful childhoods, their blocks, their fears. They are asked to be very much in the present, and to open up their feelings to the character they're working on.

If I at any point I were to inflict a specific character on someone, or a specific way of viewing that character, it would be a manipulation, and I never do that. The view of the character being played is in every instance the performer's own view. And in any case, as the person yelled out, "It's all psychodrama!" If you're not living your life with that in mind, you're coasting through. Trying to sneak by. But as they say, "The unexamined life is not worth living." If you want to sail through this existence having fun devoid of consequence, go watch TV. Your life will catch up with you sooner or later, whether you like it or not. People come to the workshops to grow, no matter what else they think they come for.

I talked earlier about the dream work I did with Anita Hall. One of the techniques she uses is to ask you to describe to her a dreamed object as if she were a Martian and had never seen or heard of the object before.

For example, if I dreamt about a refrigerator and it seemed to have some significance in the dream, Anita would say "How would you describe a refrigerator to a Martian?" and I would say to her, "A refrigerator is an electrically powered object that exists in most people's homes that's used to keep food cool and fresh. There's usually a fairly strong emotional attachment to this object since it protects one of our primary nourishment sources."

This technique allows us to discover unconscious connections to ordinary things that we might otherwise just blindly pass. It became so fertile for me that I started doing it just for fun, so now I often have conversations with a Martian visitor. One day he asked me what I did for a living. I thought about it for a while and finally said:

A.A.: I . . . I . . . (struggling for clarity) . . . I pretend I'm a human being.

MARTIAN: You pretend you're a human being?

A.A.: That's correct.

MARTIAN: Aren't you a human being?

A.A.: I am. Yes.

MARTIAN: Then why do you have to pretend you're a human being?

A.A.: People like to watch me pretend I'm a human being.

MARTIAN: Why?

A.A.: I don't know.

MARTIAN: Couldn't they just watch you be a human being without the pretending part?

A.A.: They could but they wouldn't.

MARTIAN: Why not?

A.A.: They wouldn't find me interesting.

MARTIAN: Why not?

A.A.: I . . . I'm not sure.

MARTIAN: And for this they pay you?

A.A.: They do, yes.

MARTIAN: Why would anyone pay you for pretending to be what you already are?

A.A.: They don't pay me for pretending to be what I am. They pay me for pretending to be other people.

MARTIAN: Why can't you just pretend to be you?

A.A.: I don't have to pretend to be me. I *am* me.

MARTIAN: (after a considerable pause) Are you good at pretending to be other people?

A.A.: I think so. In fact, a lot of people who do what I do, we are called actors, are better at pretending to be other people than they are at being themselves.

MARTIAN: Strange.

A.A.: I suppose it is, yes.

MARTIAN: Again I ask, why do people want to see you doing this?

A.A.: (after some thought) Because watching actors live pretend lives often gives people clues about how to live their own lives.

MARTIAN: I begin to see. You become imaginary characters, in hypothetical situations, which are then used for problem solving.

A.A.: Yes. Thank you. You said it better than I did.

MARTIAN: Who designs these problems?

A.A.: We have special people who do this. They are called writers.

MARTIAN: So you pretend to be whatever creatures these writers imagine?

A.A.: That's what I do.

MARTIAN: Are these ethical and moral people, these writers? Are they priests?

A.A.: They are occasionally ethical and moral; rarely are they priests.

MARTIAN: So, in other words, to make a living you become a pawn in someone else's assessment of the human condition for other people's amusement or possible edification.

A.A.: I suppose that's what I do, yes.

MARTIAN: A very humble work.

A.A.: Not necessarily.

MARTIAN: How so?

A.A.: Some of us are treated like gods.

MARTIAN: (shocked and incredulous) How can this be?

A.A.: Many people think we are really doing what we're pretending to do.

MARTIAN: They don't know you're pretending?

A.A.: They know we're pretending, but they pretend they don't know we're pretending.

MARTIAN: (after a great deal of mulling) You are a strange and complicated race.

A.A.: I've often thought so.

So when things get tense, when I start taking my work a bit too seriously, I remind myself that I'm only pretending to be a human being. I am happy to say that I don't take it all that seriously any longer, which doesn't seem to have affected my work too adversely.

It the final analysis, it's all improvisation. We're all tap dancing on a rubber raft. We like to think otherwise, so we plan our lives, we plot, we figure, we find careers that will guarantee us an early retirement, we look for relationships that are permanent, we fill out forms, we do scientific experiments, we write rules—all in an attempt to solidify, concretize, and control this universe of ours that refuses to be pigeon-holed, to be understood, pinned down, categorized, or even named. This magical wild horse of a universe that gallops by us and through us and around us, and every once in a while allows us to grab on to its mane for a moment or two and join in its dance, but won't be tamed, conquered, or figured out. We keep finding the smallest possible particle only to discover six months later there is a smaller one. We find suns and planets and star systems that continually defy all logic. We ask doctors for the scientific unalterable facts about our condition and when pressed to the wall they tell us they don't know the answer, they can only approximate. Psychiatrists tell us after five years, "I never promised you a rose garden." We try endlessly to make sense of the whole thing. We write down rules and regulations that are supposed to work under all conditions, it never happens. It's not possible for it to happen. You know you've found a real expert on television when they *can't* give you a definitive answer. Real experts know something about the variables, the intangibles. We are at our best, I think, when we start to let it all go. When we begin to trust the fact that millions of years of evolution have created this organism, through a lot of trial and error, and it's come up with some pretty good answers. It's all the nagging, the complaining, the plotting, the fears, the endless need to keep the universe in all its majestic chaos at bay—that with a little more thought and effort we can figure it all out, control it all, the universe, our destiny. This is what kills us, robs us of our spontaneity, our ability to *improvise*, which, as Webster's says, is *to create something on the spur of the moment with whatever material is at hand.*

That's what we're all doing, all the time, whether we know it or not. Whether we like it or not. Creating something on the spur of the moment with the materials at hand. We might just as well let the rest of it go, join the party, and dance our hearts out.

INDEX